Warren Buffett Has Spoken

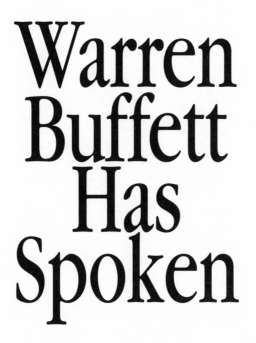

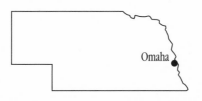

Omaha

The Question Is, Who Is Listening?

Compiled by J. Pardoe

WARREN BUFFETT HAS SPOKEN.

THE QUESTION IS,

WHO IS LISTENING?

ISBN # 0-9741934-0-2

Library of Congress Catalog Number 2003094200

Library of Congress Cataloging - in - Publication Data
Buffett, Warren.
    Warren Buffett has spoken : the question is, who is
listening? / compiled by J. Pardoe. – 1st ed.
    p. cm.
    Includes bibliographical references.
    LCCN 2003094200
    ISBN 9-9741934-0-2

    1. Buffett, Warren–Quotations. 1. Capitalists and financiers–United
States–Quotations.   I. Pardoe, J., 1967 - II. Title.

HG172.B84B8395 2003   332.6;092
                         QBI03-200540

Warren Buffett Has Spoken. The Question Is, Who Is Listening?

Before Enron declared bankruptcy in 2001 – wiping out 68 billion dollars in market value, 800 million dollars in pension funds, and thousands of jobs – Enron executives sold about 1 billion dollars worth of stock. The CEO sold an estimated 4.2 million Enron shares for 189.4 million dollars and he exercised 2.2 million options for a gain of 123.4 million dollars. From 1996 to 2000, although profitable, Enron used almost 900 subsidiaries in tax-haven countries to avoid paying income taxes in four out of those five years, realizing 381 million dollars in tax refunds.

In 2001, the former head of Global Crossing sold 9.9 million Global Crossing shares in one day and he bought a residence for 60 million dollars in cash. He ultimately cashed in approximately 734 million dollars through stock sales. Employing Arthur Andersen, the same auditor Enron used, Bermuda-based Global Crossing declared bankruptcy in 2002; thereby erasing what was once 54 billion dollars in market equity and close to 10,000 jobs.

Sadly, we live in a time when this kind of corporate conduct, especially executive enrichment at the expense of shareholders, is becoming the rule and not the exception. Fortunately, there is a CEO who is quite an exception. Despite having 99% of his net worth (476,198 shares) in the common stock of the company he runs, this CEO has never sold a company share, never owned a single option, and never split the stock. His annual salary is 100,000 dollars and he paid 31,500 dollars for his home.

This executive treats every shareholder as a partner and fellow owner of the company. His company's accounting is transparent and ethical with no overseas tax shelters. Instead, this company based in Omaha, Nebraska, paid the sum of 2.7 billion dollars in taxes to the US government in 1998 and presently employs over 145,000 Americans. This CEO's net worth of approximately 35 billion dollars makes him one of the richest men in the country, but this wealth will ultimately be bequeathed to society by his estate. Frankly, catching the Loch Ness Monster or seeing the Red Sox win the World Series seem more believable than this CEO, Warren Edward Buffett of the Berkshire Hathaway Company.

It should be remembered that Buffett had the audacity to declare the emperor wore no clothes during the height of the high tech bull market. He did not buy a single tech share when stocks such as etoys.com hit 86 dollars a share and achieved a 10 billion-dollar market capitalization.

Buffett predicted in 1999 that "equity investors currently seem wildly optimistic in their expectations about future returns...and if investor expectations become more realistic – and they almost certainly will – the market adjustment is apt to be severe, particularly in sectors in which speculation has been concentrated."

For such blasphemy and high tech abstinence, Buffett was lambasted and ridiculed as he endured savage critiques of his stewardship. Eulogies for his value investment philosophy rang throughout the financial world:

- "Buffett bombs as high-tech funds boom"
- "Warren Buffett's Annus horribilis"
- "Has the Sage of Omaha lost his marbles?"
- "Some Sage"
- "He has a stubborn streak that defies logic. In the past 10 years, there have been some outstanding discoveries and developments – cellular phones, computers, fiber optics and new wonder drugs. None are in the Berkshire portfolio."
- "A middlebrow insurance company studded with a bizarre mélange of assets, including candy stores, hamburger stands, jewelry shops, a shoemaker and a third-rate encyclopedia company."
- "Mr. Buffett, your time is up. Buy and hold investing was never as smart as Warren Buffett made it look. Today the strategy may even prove more dangerous to your portfolio."

Adding injury to insult, as the stock market was surging to new highs, Berkshire Hathaway experienced its worst year ever in 1999. Berkshire Hathaway had always been the Nebraska Cornhuskers of the New York Stock Exchange (Up until 2002, the Nebraska Cornhuskers college football team had 40 consecutive winning seasons, 33 straight years with at least 9 wins, five national championships, and a record 262 consecutive home sellouts since 1962).

In 36 years as a public holding company, Berkshire had not lost money or seen its book value decline and averaged a 27% annual return. Berkshire Hathaway shareholders hold onto stock for an average of 15 years. As a comparison, Amazon.com shareholders average one week. Attendance at the annual meeting has gone from about 13 people in 1980 to over 15,000 in 2003. However, in 1999, per share book value of the stock rose only by 0.5%, compared with 20.5% on the Standard & Poor rate. Berkshire Hathaway's stock price – which was 450 dollars in 1982 – reached an all time high of 84,000 dollars in June of 1998. Shortly thereafter, it fell out of favor and its price plummeted to 40,800 dollars in March of 2000 when the NASDAQ peaked. Berkshire Hathaway reached a low point while the rest of the stock market was soaring.

In an unprecedented mea culpa for a CEO, Warren Buffett declared in his 1999 annual report:

- "We had the worst absolute performance of my tenure and compared to the S&P, the worst relative performance as well."
- "Even Inspector Clouseau could find last year's guilty party: your Chairman."
- "What most hurt us during the year was the inferior performance of Berkshire's equity portfolio - and responsibility for that portfolio, leaving aside the small piece of it run by Lou Simpson of GEICO, is entirely mine."
- "And my grade for 1999 most assuredly is a 'D.'"

Maybe the Harvard Business School was right to reject Buffett's application in 1950.

Confronted with poor business results, a decreasing stock price, intense criticism, and a torrid market, what did Buffett do to remedy these setbacks? What dramatic changes did he make in the face of all this adversity? In the absolute worst year in his company's history, Buffett did not budge one inch from his investment and business principles. He did not panic by selling any of his holdings or buy any booming tech stocks. As the Berkshire Hathaway ship was sailing through the roughest storm in its history, Buffett kept the course, completely ignoring the siren songs coming from Wall Street. In the ultimate test of the strength of his convictions and his allegiance to his value investment principles, Buffett never compromised any of his long held beliefs and practices.

Today, amidst the ruins of the high tech gold rush, the tortoise has indeed surpassed the hare. Berkshire Hathaway enjoys restored standing with its stock price and business results and Buffett's investment philosophy has been completely vindicated.

Amazingly, even more impressive than Buffett's investment success is his stewardship as CEO. A hundred years from now, Buffett will be looked upon as the King Arthur of CEOs - a man who was an island of integrity in a sea of greed and dishonesty. His code of conduct will be remembered for its truthful accounting and rejection of executive enrichment at the expense of shareholders.

In an era when corporate executives look to their own interests first, Buffett recalls the selflessness of great leaders of the past. When Alexander the Great and his soldiers were crossing the Makran Desert, they ran out of water. His soldiers were dying of thirst as they advanced under the burning sun. Some of Alexander's lieutenants managed to obtain some water from a passing caravan and they brought a small pouch of water to their general. Alexander asked "Is there enough water for my men and me?" "Only you, sir," they replied. Alexander poured the water on the ground as he told his lieutenants, "I will drink when my soldiers drink."

What other CEO has ever made this Alexandrian pledge? "What we promise you - along with more modest gains

– is that during your ownership of Berkshire, you will fare just as Charlie [Munger] and I do. If you suffer, we will suffer; if we prosper, so will you. And we will not break this bond by introducing compensation arrangements that give us a greater participation in the upside than the downside. We further promise you that our personal fortunes will remain overwhelmingly concentrated in Berkshire shares: We will not ask you to invest with us and then put our own money elsewhere."

Buffett has set a precedent for ethics that, hopefully, future CEOs will emulate. His refusal to engage in unprincipled behavior, coupled with his investment record, serves as an important lesson that a CEO who acts with integrity can still succeed.

Buffett's insight shows that one does not need a high IQ to be a good investor. As Buffett makes evident, MBAs and knowledge of esoteric financial theories and formulas are not required to be successful in the stock market. Rather, he shows what one needs is rational behavior and discipline. Buffett dispels the notion that investing in the stock market is a black magic only high priests (money management professionals, brokers, financial analysts, academicians) can perform. By following Buffett's wisdom found in the quotes in this book, one will have an intellectual framework for behaving in the stock market.

Mark Twain, Will Rogers, and Confucius were men who became famous for their ability to enlighten, inspire, and amuse with a quote. As you will soon see, Warren Buffett's quotations belong in the company of these giants.

Buffett's greatest legacy will be his code of conduct that he adheres to as an investor and CEO. The following quotations are for future generations to read and, most importantly, think about. These quotes are akin to holy financial scripture and should be recited by every stock market investor before making an investment and by every CEO starting his stewardship.

Enjoy the epiphany!
J. Pardoe

Table of Contents

Business & Investment Philosophy

"Though we continue to be unwilling to talk about specific stocks, we freely discuss our business and investment philosophy. I benefited enormously from the intellectual generosity of Ben Graham, the greatest teacher in the history of finance, and I believe it appropriate to pass along what I learned from him, even if that creates new and able investment competitors for Berkshire just as Ben's teachings did for him."

"If there's one key to what I do it's that I look at every share of stock as being a part of a business. So if I'm going to buy 100 shares of General Motors or General Electric or whatever it may be, I try and look at what the whole business is selling for and then do I want to buy this tiny little piece of that business at that price? That means I think about the business. I don't think about the price action of the stock or I don't think about what people are saying they're going to earn next quarter or anything of that sort, or look at charts. I just try and look at the business. Now, what does that mean? It means I have to understand the business. A lot of businesses I can't understand. I can understand Gillette. I can understand Coca-Cola. I can understand Wrigley's Chewing Gum. I mean those are things that I can understand and when I say I can understand it, it means I have a pretty good idea of what they're going to look like 10 or 15 years from now. That's understanding a business."

"With Coke I can come up with a very rational figure for the cash it will generate in the future. But with the top 10 Internet companies, how much cash will they produce over the next 25 years? If you say you don't know, then you don't know what it is worth and you are speculating, not investing. All I know is that I don't know, and if I don't know, I don't invest."

"In my opinion, investment success will not be produced by arcane formulae, computer programs or signals flashed by the price behavior of stocks and markets. Rather an investor will succeed by coupling good business judgment with an ability to insulate his thoughts and behavior from the super-contagious emotions that swirl about the marketplace."

"You can't do well in investments unless you think independently."

"I'm just not terribly affected by the fact that the crowds are agreeing with me or disagreeing with me. I'll do whatever my own sense tells me. The real trick is to just sit and think."

"We derive no comfort because important people, vocal people, or great numbers of people agree with us. Nor do we derive comfort if they don't."

"None of this means, however, that a business or stock is an intelligent purchase simply because it is unpopular; a contrarian approach is just as foolish as a follow-the-crowd strategy. What's required is thinking rather than polling."

"Ben used to say you're neither right nor wrong because people agree with you. You're right because your facts and your reasoning are right."

"Following Ben's teachings, Charlie and I let our marketable equities tell us by their operating results - not by their daily, or even yearly, price quotations - whether our investments are successful. The market may ignore business success for a while, but eventually will confirm it. As Ben said: 'In the short run, the market is a voting machine but in the long run it is a weighing machine.'"

"Severe change and exceptional returns usually don't mix. Most investors, of course, behave as if just the opposite were true. That is, they usually confer the highest price-earnings ratios on exotic-sounding businesses that hold out the promise of feverish change. That prospect lets investors fantasize about future profitability rather than face today's business realities. For such investor-dreamers, any blind date is preferable to one with the girl next door, no matter how desirable she may be."

"I should emphasize that, as citizens, Charlie and I welcome change: Fresh ideas, new products, innovative processes and the like cause our country's standard of living to rise, and that's clearly good. As investors, however, our reaction to a fermenting industry is much like our attitude toward space exploration: We applaud the endeavor but prefer to skip the ride."

"In studying the investments we have made in both subsidiary companies and common stocks, you will see that we favor businesses and industries unlikely to experience major change. The reason for that is simple: Making either type of purchase, we are searching for operations that we believe are virtually certain to possess enormous competitive strength ten or twenty years from now. A fast-changing industry environment may offer the chance for huge wins, but it precludes the certainty we seek."

"The Dilly bar is more certain to be around in 10 years than a single software application."

"We try to stick to businesses we believe we understand. That means they must be relatively simple and stable in character. If a business is complex or subject to constant change, we're not smart enough to predict future cash flows. Incidentally, that shortcoming doesn't bother us. What counts for most people in investing is not how much they know, but rather how realistically they define what they don't know. An investor needs to do very few things right as long as he or she avoids big mistakes. Second, and equally important, we insist on a margin of safety in our purchase price. If we calculate the value of a common stock to be only slightly higher than its price, we're not interested in buying. We believe this margin-of-safety principle, so strongly emphasized by Ben Graham, to be the cornerstone of investment success."

"If you only buy into things you understand, and then you are disciplined about what you will pay when you buy into them, you can't lose money. We've never lost a lot of money. I mean, we've missed all kinds of things on the upside but the reason we don't lose money is because we think of ourselves as buying businesses and not stocks. And we just pay an intelligent price for the business."

"Rule No. 1: Never lose money. Rule No. 2: Never forget rule No. 1."

"Experience, however, indicates that the best business returns are usually achieved by companies that are doing something quite similar today to what they were doing five or ten years ago. That is no argument for managerial complacency. Businesses always have opportunities to improve service, product lines, manufacturing techniques, and the like, and obviously these opportunities should be seized. But a business that constantly encounters major change also encounters many chances for major error. Furthermore, economic terrain that is forever shifting violently is ground on which it is difficult to build a fortress-like business franchise. Such a franchise is usually the key to sustained high returns."

"The test of a franchise is what a smart guy with a lot of money could do to it if he tried. If you gave me a billion dollars, and you gave me first draft pick of 50 business managers and 50 journalists, and you said, 'Go take the Wall Street Journal apart,' I would hand you back the billion dollars. There are some businesses that have very large moats around them. Those are the businesses you want."

"If you gave me $100 billion and said take away the soft drink leadership of Coca-Cola in the world, I'd give it back to you and say it can't be done."

"The fact is that newspaper, television, and magazine properties have begun to resemble businesses more than franchises in their economic behavior. Let's take a quick look at the characteristics separating these two classes of enterprise, keeping in mind, however, that many operations fall in some middle ground and can be best described as weak franchises or strong businesses. An economic franchise arises from a product or service that: (1) is needed or desired; (2) is thought by its customers to have no close substitute and; (3) is not subject to price regulation. The existence of all three conditions will be demonstrated by a company's ability to regularly price its product or service aggressively and thereby to earn high rates of return on capital. Moreover, franchises can tolerate mismanagement. Inept managers may diminish a franchise's profitability, but they cannot inflict mortal damage. In contrast, 'a business' earns exceptional profits only if it is the low-cost operator or if supply of its product or service is tight. Tightness in supply usually does not last long. With superior management, a company may maintain its status as a low-cost operator for a much longer time, but even then unceasingly faces the possibility of competitive attack. And a business, unlike a franchise, can be killed by poor management."

"We don't intentionally go into a business that we think will change in a big way. We look for a moat. A business is like a castle. What kind of protective moat do you have? See's [Candy] has widened its moat every year. Other businesses are trying to take your castle. We think our businesses have solid moats and they're widening them."

"I won't dwell on other glamorous businesses that dramatically changed our lives but concurrently failed to deliver rewards to U.S. investors: the manufacture of radios and televisions, for example. But I will draw a lesson from these businesses: The key to investing is not assessing how much an industry is going to affect society, or how much it will grow, but rather determining the competitive advantage of any given company and, above all, the durability of that advantage. The products or services that have wide, sustainable moats around them are the ones that deliver rewards to investors."

"Look for the durability of the franchise. The most important thing to me is figuring out how big a moat there is around the business. What I love, of course, is a big castle and a big moat with piranhas and crocodiles."

"Obviously all businesses change to some extent. Today, See's [Candy] is different in many ways from what it was in 1972 when we bought it: It offers a different assortment of candy, employs different machinery and sells through different distribution channels. But the reasons why people today buy boxed chocolates, and why they buy them from us rather than from someone else, are virtually unchanged from what they were in the 1920s when the See family was building the business. Moreover, these motivations are not likely to change over the next 20 years, or even 50. We look for similar predictability in marketable securities."

"The goal of each investor should be to create a portfolio (in effect, a 'company') that will deliver him or her the highest possible look-through earnings a decade or so from now. An approach of this kind will force the investor to think about long-term business prospects rather than short-term stock market prospects, a perspective likely to improve results. It's true, of course, that, in the long run, the scoreboard for investment decisions is market price. But prices will be determined by future earnings. In investing, just as in baseball, to put runs on the scoreboard one must watch the playing field, not the scoreboard."

"What's nice is that sound investing can make you very wealthy if you're not in too big a hurry. And it never makes you poor – which is even better."

"We have no idea – and never have had – whether the market is going to go up, down, or sideways in the near-or intermediate-term future. What we do know, however, is that occasional outbreaks of those two super-contagious diseases, fear and greed, will forever occur in the investment community. The timing of these epidemics will be unpredictable. And the market aberrations produced by them will be equally unpredictable, both as to duration and degree. Therefore, we never try to anticipate the arrival or departure of either disease. Our goal is more modest: we simply attempt to be fearful when others are greedy and to be greedy only when others are fearful."

"An intellectual framework for investing and a temperamental model, the ability to stand back and not be influenced by a crowd, not be fearful if stocks go down. When proper temperament joins with proper intellectual framework, then you get rational behavior."

"Success in investing doesn't correlate with I.Q. once you're above the level of 25. Once you have ordinary intelligence, what you need is the temperament to control the urges that get other people into trouble in investing."

"To be sure, an investor needs some general understanding of business economics as well as the ability to think independently to reach a well-founded positive conclusion. But the investor does not need brilliance nor blinding insights."

"Beware of past-performance 'proofs' in finance: if history books were the key to riches, the Forbes 400 would consist of librarians."

"Future profitability of the industry will be determined by current competitive characteristics, not past ones. Most managers have been slow to recognize this. It's not only generals that prefer to fight the last war. Most business and investment analysis also comes from the rear-view mirror."

"I always find it extraordinary that so many studies are made of price and volume behavior, the stuff of chartists. Can you imagine buying an entire business simply because the price of the business had been marked up substantially last week and the week before? Of course, the reason a lot of studies are made of these price and volume variables is that now, in the age of computers, there are almost endless data available about them. It isn't necessarily because such studies have any utility; it's simply that the data are there and academicians have worked hard to learn the mathematical skills needed to manipulate them. Once these skills are acquired, it seems sinful not to use them, even if the usage has no utility or negative utility. As a friend said, to a man with a hammer, everything looks like a nail."

"We just try to buy businesses with good to superb under-lying economics, run by honest and able people, and buy them at sensible prices. That's all I'm trying to do."

"The fact that it's so simple makes people reluctant to teach it. If you've gone and gotten a Ph.D and spent years learning how to do all kinds of tough things mathematically, to have it come back to this – it's like studying for the priesthood and finding out that the Ten Commandments were all you needed."

"Read Ben Graham and Phil Fisher, read annual reports, but don't do equations with Greek letters in them."

"Adding many converts to the value approach will perforce narrow the spreads between price and value. I can only tell you that the secret has been out for 50 years, ever since Ben Graham and Dave Dodd wrote Security Analysis, yet I have seen no trend toward value investing in the 35 years that I've practiced it. There seems to be some perverse human characteristic that likes to make easy things difficult. The academic world, if anything, has actually backed away from the teaching of value investing over the last 30 years. It's likely to continue that way. Ships will sail around the world but the Flat Earth Society will flourish. There will continue to be wide discrepancies between price and value in the marketplace, and those who read their Graham & Dodd will continue to prosper."

"We think the very term 'value investing' is redundant. What is 'investing' if it is not the act of seeking value at least sufficient to justify the amount paid? Consciously paying more for a stock than its calculated value - in the hope of that it can be sold for a still-higher price - should be labeled speculation (which is neither illegal, immoral nor – in our view – financially fattening)."

"Think of investing as owning a business and not as buying something that wiggles around in price."

"The professional in almost any field achieves a result which is significantly above what the layman in aggregate achieves. It's not true in money management."

"You have a profession where the practitioners as a whole can add nothing to what you can do yourself."

"Every one of these [list of 37 former investment-banking firms] has disappeared. This happened while the volume of the New York Stock Exchange multiplied fifteenfold. All these companies had people with high IQs working for them, who worked ungodly hard and had intense desires for success and money. They all thought they would be leaders on Wall Street. You think about that. How could they get a result like that? These were bright people; they had their own money in their businesses. I'll tell you how they did it: mindless imitation of their peers. I don't get great ideas talking to people. I never talk to brokers or analysts. You have to think about things yourself. These people all gave advice to companies about how they should run their businesses. You know, Wall Street is the only place that people ride to in a Rolls Royce to get advice from those who take the subway."

"It has been helpful to me to have the tens of thousands turned out of business schools taught that it didn't do any good to think."

"We will continue to ignore political and economic forecasts, which are an expensive distraction for many investors and businessmen. Thirty years ago, no one could have foreseen the huge expansion of the Vietnam War, wage and price controls, two oil shocks, the resignation of a president, the dissolution of the Soviet Union, a one-day drop in the Dow of 508 points, or treasury bill yields fluctuating between 2.8% and 17.4%. But, surprise - none of these blockbuster events made the slightest dent in Ben Graham's investment principles. Nor did they render unsound the negotiated purchases of fine businesses at sensible prices. Imagine the cost to us, then, if we had let a fear of unknowns cause us to defer or alter the deployment of capital. Indeed, we have usually made our best purchases when apprehensions about some macro event were at a peak. Fear is the foe of the faddist, but the friend of the fundamentalist. A different set of major shocks is sure to occur in the next 30 years. We will neither try to predict these nor to profit from them. If we can identify businesses similar to those we have purchased in the past, external surprises will have little effect on our long-term results."

"In any business, there are going to be all kinds of factors that happen next week, next month, next year, and
so forth. But the really important thing is to be in the
right businesses. The classic case for me is Coca-Cola,
which went public in 1919. They initially sold stock at
$40 per share. The next year it went down to $19. Sugar
prices had changed dramatically after World War I. But if
you bought a share when it came public and held that
share reinvesting all your dividends, that share would be
worth $1.8 million today. We have had depressions. We
have had wars. Sugar prices have gone up and down. A
million things have happened. How much more fruitful
is it for us to think about whether the product is likely
to sustain itself and its economics than to try to be
questioning whether to jump in or out of the stock."

"A second argument is made that there are just too many
question marks about the near future; wouldn't it be
better to wait until things clear up a bit? You know
the prose: 'Maintain buying reserves until current
uncertainties are resolved,' etc. Before reaching for that
crutch, face up to two unpleasant facts: The future is
never clear; you pay a very high price in the stock
market for a cheery consensus. Uncertainty actually is
the friend of the buyer of long-term values."

"We try to price, rather than time, purchases. In our view, it is folly to forego buying shares in an outstanding business whose long-term future is predictable, because of short-term worries about an economy or a stock market that we know to be unpredictable. Why scrap an informed decision because of an uninformed guess?"

"We purchased National Indemnity in 1967, See's in 1972, Buffalo News in 1977, Nebraska Furniture Mart in 1983, and Scott Fetzer in 1986 because those are the years they became available and because we thought the prices they carried were acceptable. In each case, we pondered what the business was likely to do, not what the Dow, the Fed, or the economy might do. If we see this approach as making sense in the purchase of businesses in their entirety, why should we change tack when we are purchasing small pieces of wonderful businesses in the stock market?"

"We try to buy into businesses with favorable long-term economics. Our goal is to find an outstanding business at a sensible price, not a mediocre business at a bargain price. Charlie and I have found that making silk purses out of silk is the best that we can do; with sow's ears, we fail. (It must be noted that your Chairman, always a quick study, required only 20 years to recognize how important it was to buy good businesses. In the interim, I searched for 'bargains' - and had the misfortune to find some. My punishment was an education in the economics of short-line farm implement manufacturers, third-place department stores, and New England textile manufacturers)."

"Investors need to avoid the negatives of buying fads, crummy companies, and timing the market."

"When buying companies or common stocks, we look for first-class businesses accompanied by first-class managements."

"It's far better to buy a wonderful company at a fair price than a fair company at a wonderful price."

"We select our marketable equity securities in much the same way we would evaluate a business for acquisition in its entirety. We want the business to be (1) one that we can understand, (2) with favorable long-term prospects, (3) operated by honest and competent people, and (4) available at a very attractive price. We ordinarily make no attempt to buy equities for anticipated favorable stock price behavior in the short term. In fact, if their business experience continues to satisfy us, we welcome lower market prices of stocks we own as an opportunity to acquire even more of a good thing at a better price."

"The stock market is there to serve you and not instruct you on how to buy. Investors should love volatility in the market. You like huge swings in the market because that means more stocks will be mispriced. It opens up opportunities."

"In the frontispiece to Security Analysis, Ben Graham and Dave Dodd quoted Horace: 'Many shall be restored that now are fallen and many shall fall that are now in honor.' Fifty-two years after I first read those lines, my appreciation for what they say about business and investments continues to grow."

"Great investment opportunities come around when excellent companies are surrounded by unusual circumstances that cause the stock to be misappraised."

"We love to buy into what is clearly a great franchise when for one reason or another, people are disappointed."

"Berkshire buys when the lemmings are heading the other way."

"The market like the Lord, helps those who help themselves. But, unlike the Lord, the market does not forgive those who know not what they do."

"For some reason, people take their cues from price action rather than values. What doesn't work is when you start doing things that you don't understand or because they worked last week for someone else. The worst reason in the world to buy a stock is because it's going up or sell a stock because it's going down."

"I don't think at all about the stock market or a given stock in the short term. We look at stocks as pieces of businesses. That is crucial in my view to the investing process, not to think about stocks as something that goes up or down, but think about the business you own."

"All the ticker tells me is the price. It doesn't tell me anything about the business."

"If the business does well, the stock eventually follows."

"The nine most important words ever written about investing are 'Investing is most intelligent when it is most businesslike.'"

"If you're an investor, you're looking on what the asset is going to do. If you're a speculator, you're commonly focusing on what the price of the object is going to do, and that's not our game. We feel that if we're right about the business, we're going to make a lot of money, and if we're wrong about the business, we don't have any hopes of making money."

"Price is what you pay. Value is what you get."

"The best test of whether you're really investing or not is to say to yourself right before you put in the order to buy a stock, 'If they closed down the stock market for three years tomorrow, would I be happy owning this?' That will tell you if you're gambling with a stock or investing in a business."

"I never attempt to make money on the stock market. I buy on the assumption that they could close the market the next day and not reopen it for five years."

"Our new commitments are not based on a judgment about short-term prospects for the stock market. Rather, they reflect an opinion about long-term business prospects for specific companies. We do not have, never have had, and never will have an opinion about where the stock market, interest rates, or business activity will be a year from now."

"All we worry about is the business. It's what the business is doing that counts."

"I am not a macro guy. I don't think about it. If Alan Greenspan is whispering in one ear and Bob Rubin in the other, I don't care at all. I'm watching the businesses."

"When investing, we view ourselves as business analysts – not as market analysts, not as macroeconomic analysts, and not even as security analysts."

"I don't usually pay much attention to other people's forecasts. I look at stocks, not markets. We make no attempt to time markets. I am a market agnostic."

"If you can detach yourself from the emotions of the market, you are going to get a chance periodically to do something intelligent - not very often, but periodically. As far as I am concerned the market doesn't exist. It is there only as a reference point to check to see if anybody is offering to do anything foolish. When we invest in stocks we invest in businesses. You simply have to behave according to what is rational rather than according to what is fashionable."

"The fact is that markets behave in ways, sometimes for a very long stretch, that are not linked to value. Sooner or later, though, value counts."

"You know, the 17 years from 1964 to 1991, the Dow moved not at all and the country grew out. So we have this history where the market gets out of sync with the business world for long periods of time and usually it's because it overshoots in one direction and it overcorrects in the other direction. And certainly we had an overshooting. So it would not surprise me if there was a long period of either stagnation or whatever it may be in the market, even though business may be making some progress. But eventually stocks will behave and sync with business."

"I look at businesses. The markets are a mystery to me and always have been. The question is, can you make money without predicting the market? I think you can."

"We've long felt that the only value of stock forecasters is to make fortune tellers look good. Even now, Charlie and I continue to believe that short-term market forecasts are poison and should be kept locked up in a safe place, away from children and also from grown-ups who behave in the market like children."

"We believe that short-term forecasts of stock or bond prices are useless. Forecasts may tell you a great deal about the forecaster; they tell you nothing about the future."

"It is impossible to predict precisely what will develop in investment or speculative markets, and you should be wary of any who claim precision."

"As far as I am concerned, the stock market doesn't exist. If Fed chairman Alan Greenspan were to whisper to me what his monetary policy was going to be over the next two years, I wouldn't change a thing. Lethargy bordering on sloth remains the cornerstone of our investment style."

"Our portfolio shows little change: We continue to make more money when snoring than when active. Inactivity strikes us as intelligent behavior. Neither we nor most business managers would dream of feverishly trading highly-profitable subsidiaries because a small move in the Federal Reserve's discount rate was predicted or because some Wall Street pundit had reversed his views on the market. Why, then, should we behave differently with our minority positions in wonderful businesses? The art of investing in public companies successfully is little different from the art of successfully acquiring subsidiaries. In each case you simply want to acquire, at a sensible price, a business with excellent economics and able, honest management. Thereafter, you need only monitor whether these qualities are being preserved."

"We like to buy. Selling, however, is a different story. There, our pace of activity resembles that forced upon a traveler who found himself stuck in tiny Podunk's only hotel. With no T.V. in his room, he faced an evening of boredom. But his spirits soared when he spied a book on the night table entitled 'Things to do in Podunk.' Opening it, he found just a single sentence: 'You're doing it.'"

"One of my quirks is that I like to keep things. The best stock to buy is one you are never going to sell."

"We can be very patient. (No matter how great the talent or effort, some things just take time: you can't produce a baby in one month by getting nine women pregnant)."

"Our stay-put behavior reflects our view that the stock market serves as a relocation center at which money is moved from the active to the patient. (With tongue only partly in cheek, I suggest that recent events indicate that the much-maligned 'idle rich' have received a bad rap: They have maintained or increased their wealth while many of the 'energetic rich'– aggressive real estate operators, corporate acquirers, oil drillers, etc. have seen their fortunes disappear)."

"If you aren't willing to own a stock for ten years, don't even think about owning it for ten minutes."

"In fact, when we own portions of outstanding businesses with outstanding managements, our favorite holding period is forever. We are just the opposite of those who hurry to sell and book profits when companies perform well but who tenaciously hang on to businesses that disappoint. Peter Lynch aptly likens such behavior to cutting the flowers and watering the weeds."

"Nor do we think many others can achieve long-term investment success by flitting from flower to flower. Indeed, we believe that according the name 'investors' to institutions that trade actively is like calling someone who repeatedly engages in one-night stands a romantic."

"You might think that institutions, with their large staffs of highly-paid and experienced investment professionals, would be a force for stability and reason in financial markets. They are not: stocks heavily owned and constantly monitored by institutions have often been among the most inappropriately valued. Ben Graham told a story 40 years ago that illustrates why investment professionals behave as they do: An oil prospector, moving to his heavenly reward, was met by St. Peter with bad news. 'You're qualified for residence', said St. Peter, 'but, as you can see, the compound reserved for oil men is packed. There's no way to squeeze you in.' After thinking a moment, the prospector asked if he might say just four words to the present occupants. That seemed harmless to St. Peter, so the prospector cupped his hands and yelled, 'Oil discovered in hell.' Immediately the gate to the compound opened and all of the oil men marched out to head for the nether regions. Impressed, St. Peter invited the prospector to move in and make himself comfortable. The prospector paused. 'No,' he said, 'I think I'll go along with the rest of the boys. There might be some truth to that rumor after all.'"

"They are fond of saying that the small investor has no chance in a market now dominated by the erratic behavior of the big boys. This conclusion is dead wrong: Such markets are ideal for any investor – small or large – so long as he sticks to his investment knitting. Volatility caused by money managers who speculate irrationally with huge sums will offer the true investor more chances to make intelligent investment moves. He can be hurt by such volatility only if he is forced, by either financial or psychological pressures, to sell at untoward times."

"One of the ironies of the stock market is the emphasis on activity. Brokers, using terms such as 'marketability' and 'liquidity', sing the praises of companies with high share turnover (those who cannot fill your pocket will confidently fill your ear). But investors should understand that what is good for the croupier is not good for the customer. A hyperactive stock market is the pickpocket of enterprise."

"As this is written, little fear is visible in Wall Street. Instead, euphoria prevails – and why not? What could be more exhilarating than to participate in a bull market in which the rewards to owners of businesses become gloriously uncoupled from the plodding performances of the businesses themselves. Unfortunately, however, stocks can't outperform businesses indefinitely."

"Investors making purchases in an overheated market need to recognize that it may often take an extended period for the value of even an outstanding company to catch up with the price they paid."

"The most common cause of low prices is pessimism – some times pervasive, some times specific to a company or industry. We want to do business in such an environment, not because we like pessimism but because we like the prices it produces. It's optimism that is the enemy of the rational buyer. None of this means, however, that a business or stock is an intelligent purchase because it is unpopular; a contrarian approach is just as foolish as a follow-the-crowd strategy. What's required is thinking rather than polling. Unfortunately, Bertrand Russell's observation about life in general applies with unusual force in the financial world: 'Most men would rather die than think. Many do.'"

"A short quiz: If you plan to eat hamburgers throughout your life and are not a cattle producer, should you wish for higher or lower prices for beef? Likewise, if you are going to buy a car from time to time but are not an auto manufacturer, should you prefer higher or lower car prices? These questions, of course, answer themselves. But now for the final exam: If you expect to be a net saver during the next five years, should you hope for a higher or lower stock market during that period? Many investors get this one wrong. Even though they are going to be net buyers of stocks for many years to come, they are elated when stock prices rise and depressed when they fall. In effect, they rejoice because prices have risen for the 'hamburgers' they will soon be buying. This reaction makes no sense. Only those who will be sellers of equities in the near future should be happy at seeing stocks rise. Prospective purchasers should much prefer sinking prices."

"So smile when you read a headline that says 'Investors lose as market falls.' Edit it in your mind to 'Disinvestors lose as market falls – but investors gain.' Though writers often forget this truism, there is a buyer for every seller and what hurts one necessarily helps the other. (As they say in golf matches:'Every putt makes someone happy'). We gained enormously from the low prices placed on many equities and businesses in the 1970s and 1980s. Markets that then were hostile to investment transients were friendly to those taking up permanent residence."

"Time is the friend of the wonderful business, the enemy of the mediocre."

"Someone's sitting in the shade today because someone planted a tree a long time ago."

"Most people get interested in stocks when everyone else is. The time to get interested is when no one else is. You can't buy what is popular and do well."

"Whether you achieve outstanding results will depend on the effort and intellect you apply to your investments, as well as on the amplitudes of stock-market folly that prevail during your investing career. The sillier the market's behavior, the greater the opportunity for the business-like investor. Follow Graham and you will profit from folly rather than participate in it."

"Ben Graham, my friend and teacher, long ago described the mental attitude toward market fluctuations that I believe to be most conducive to investment success. He said that you should imagine market quotations as coming from a remarkably accommodating fellow named Mr. Market who is your partner in a private business. Without fail, Mr. Market appears daily and names a price at which he will either buy your interest or sell you his. Even though the business that the two of you own may have economic characteristics that are stable, Mr. Market's quotations will be anything but. For, sad to say, the poor fellow has incurable emotional problems. At times he feels euphoric and can see only the favorable factors affecting the business. When in that mood, he names a very high buy-sell price because he fears that you will snap up his interest and rob him of imminent gains. At other times he is depressed and can see nothing but trouble ahead for both the business and the world. On these occasions he will name a very low price, since he is terrified that you will unload your interest on him. Mr. Market has another endearing characteristic: He doesn't mind being ignored. If his quotation is uninteresting to you today, he will be back with a new one tomorrow. Transactions are strictly at your option. Under these conditions, the more manic-depressive his behavior, the better for you.

But, like Cinderella at the ball, you must heed one warning or everything will turn into pumpkins and mice: Mr. Market is there to serve you, not to guide you. It is his pocketbook, not his wisdom, that you will find useful. If he shows up some day in a particularly foolish mood, you are free to either ignore him or to take advantage of him, but it will be disastrous if you fall under his influence. Indeed, if you aren't certain that you understand and can value your business far better than Mr. Market, you don't belong in the game. As they say in poker, 'If you've been in the game 30 minutes and you don't know who the patsy is, you're the patsy.' Ben's Mr. Market allegory may seem out-of-date in today's investment world, in which most professionals and academicians talk of efficient markets, dynamic hedging and betas. Their interest in such matters is understandable, since techniques shrouded in mystery clearly have value to the purveyor of investment advice. After all, what witch doctor has ever achieved fame and fortune by simply advising 'take two aspirins'?"

"Mentally we're always buying businesses. It's just that sometimes we can buy all of them and sometimes we can only buy little pieces of them. Unfortunately, I would say the market for businesses is far more efficient than the stock market. It is much more difficult to find wide discrepancies in price and values when you engage in a negotiated transaction with some seller than it is when you deal on the floor of the stock exchange. That is, when the price of a stock is determined by the most emotional or the most greedy, the person that day affected by all the forces that affect him, it's a lot different than going out to some guy who owns a television station in Kalamazoo and telling him that because the Dow is down 20 points today he ought to sell the station to you a lot cheaper. You get into the real world when you deal with businesses. But in stocks everyone is thinking about relative prices. So when the price of companies goes down 40%, the price of the Washington Post Co. goes down 40%. All these people in the market are making decisions, but they're not thinking of the value of the business. When we bought 8% or 9% of the Washington Post in one month, not one person who selling stock to us was thinking, I'm selling 400$ million for $80 million. They don't think that way. They had all these nonsensical reasons: Communication stocks were going down, other people were selling. If you want to do business with somebody, do business

with someone who operates on nonsensical reasons.
And people in the private market generally don't."

"I'm convinced that there is much inefficiency in the
market. These Graham and Doddsville investors have
successfully exploited gaps between price and value.
When the price of a stock can be influenced by a 'herd'
on Wall Street with prices set at the margin by the most
emotional person, or the greediest person, or the most
depressed person, it is hard to argue that the market
always prices rationally. In fact, market prices are
frequently nonsensical."

"Today we have $15 billion in cash. Do I like getting 5% on it? No. But I like the $15 billion, and I don't want to put it in something that's not going to give it back and then some. The nature of markets is that at times they offer extraordinary values and at other times you have to have the discipline to wait."

"You do things when the opportunities come along. I've had periods in my life when I've had a bundle of ideas come along, and I've had long dry spells. If I get an idea next week, I'll do something. If not, I won't do a damn thing."

"I know what I know, and I know what I don't know pretty well. I've got a circle of competence. It may be a small one, but within that circle I'm perfectly willing to act and act fast and act big."

"In the summer of 1979, when equities looked cheap to me, I wrote a Forbes article entitled 'You pay a very high price in the stock market for a cheery consensus.' At that time skepticism and disappointment prevailed, and my point was that investors should be glad of the fact, since pessimism drives down prices to truly attractive levels. Now, however, we have a very cheery consensus. That does not necessarily mean this is the wrong time to buy stocks: Corporate America is now earning far more money than it was just a few years ago, and in the presence of lower interest rates, every dollar of earnings becomes more valuable. Today's price levels, though, have materially eroded the 'margin of safety' that Ben Graham identified as the cornerstone of intelligent investing."

"Investors should remember that their scorecard is not computed using Olympic-diving methods: Degree-of-difficulty doesn't count. If you are right about a business whose value is largely dependent on a single key factor that is both easy to understand and enduring, the payoff is the same as if you had correctly analyzed an investment alternative characterized by many constantly shifting and complex variables."

"After 25 years of buying and supervising a great variety of businesses, Charlie and I have not learned how to solve difficult business problems. What we have learned is to avoid them. To the extent that we have been successful, it is because we concentrated on identifying one-foot hurdles that we could step over rather than because we acquired any ability to clear seven-footers. The finding may seem unfair, but in both business and investments it is usually far more profitable to simply stick with the easy and obvious than it is to resolve the difficult."

"You shouldn't own common stocks if a 50% decrease in their market value in a short period of time would cause you acute distress."

"It bothers us not at all if a stock drops 50% – in fact we like it – it means we can buy more at a lower price. We look to what's happening within the business to gauge our success, not the market."

"For example, I haven't had a quote on See's Candy since we bought it in 1972 but I know the business is doing OK. I don't need a quote on it. And, you know, people manage to live through Saturday and Sunday without getting quotes on their stocks. If the stock exchange closed for a year or two, for a real investor, it wouldn't make any difference."

"You should entirely avoid owning stocks if a crashing market would lead you to panic and sell. Selling fine businesses on 'scary' news is usually a bad decision. Robert Woodruff, the business genius who built Coca-Cola over many decades and who owned a huge position in the company, was once asked when it might be a good time to sell Coke stock. Woodruff had a simple answer: 'I don't know. I've never sold any.'"

"Stocks are simple. All you do is buy shares in a great business for less than the business is intrinsically worth, with managers of the highest integrity and ability. Then you own those shares forever."

Diversification

"Keynes essentially said don't try and figure out what the market is doing. Figure out businesses you understand, and concentrate. Diversification is protection against ignorance, but if you don't feel ignorant, the need for it goes down drastically."

"If you are a know-something investor, able to understand business economics and to find five to ten sensibly-priced companies that possess important long-term competitive advantages, conventional diversification makes no sense for you. It is apt simply to hurt your results and increase your risk. I cannot understand why an investor of that sort elects to put money into a business that is his 20th favorite rather than simply adding that money to his top choices – the businesses he understands best and that present the least risk, along with the greatest profit potential. In the words of the prophet Mae West: 'Too much of a good thing can be wonderful.'"

"Our policy is to concentrate holdings. We try to avoid buying a little of this or that when we are only lukewarm about the business or its price. When we are convinced as to attractiveness, we believe in buying worthwhile amounts."

"I can't be involved in 50 or 75 things. That's a Noah's Ark way of investing. You end up with a zoo that way. I like to put meaningful amounts of money in a few things."

"I put a billion dollars in Coca-Cola because I understood the business. I had been drinking it for 55 years and finally decided they had something."

"The strategy we've adopted precludes our following standard diversification dogma. Many pundits would therefore say the strategy must be riskier than that employed by more conventional investors. We disagree. We believe that a policy of portfolio concentration may well decrease risk if it raises, as it should, both the intensity with which an investor thinks about a business and the comfort-level he must feel with its economic characteristics before buying into it. In stating this opinion, we define risk, using dictionary terms as 'the possibility of loss or injury.'"

"The less you know, the more you have to own. Diversification is a protection against mistakes or ignorance."

"If my own family's fortune for the next 30 years were dependent on the income from a group of businesses, I can assure you that I'd rather pick three businesses from those we own than own a diversified group of 50."

"The great fortunes in this country weren't built on a portfolio of 50 companies. They were built by someone who identified one wonderful business."

"Billy Rose used to say that if you have a harem of 100 girls, you never get to know any of them very well. The trick is to know a lot about what you own, and you don't need to own a lot of things. The great businesses of the world don't own that many things."

"I tell people if they got when they were 21, a card with 20 punches on it. And every time they made an investment decision, they used up a punch. And when the 20 punches were gone, they were done, they'd make a lot of money, because they would think a long time before they make any decision. They would think a long time before they buy a car or buy a house or all that. But many people do buy a stock, just because somebody mentioned it that day, particularly if stocks have been going up."

"The trick is just to do a few things."

"I believe every business school graduate should sign an unbreakable contract promising not to make more than 20 major decisions in a lifetime. In a 40-year career you would make a decision every two years."

"Charlie and I decided long ago that in an investment lifetime it's just too hard to make hundreds of smart decisions. That judgment became ever more compelling as Berkshire's capital mushroomed and the universe of investments that could significantly affect our results shrank dramatically. Therefore, we adopted a strategy that required our being smart – and not too smart at that – only a very few times. Indeed, we'll now settle for one good idea a year (Charlie says it's my turn)."

"If my universe of business possibilities was limited, say to private companies in Omaha, I would, first, try to assess the long-term economic characteristics of each business; second, assess the quality of the people in charge of running it; and, third, try to buy into a few of the best operations at a sensible price. I certainly would not wish to own an equal part of every business in town. Why, then, should Berkshire take a different tack when dealing with the larger universe of public companies? And since finding great businesses and outstanding managers is so difficult, why should we discard proven products? (I was tempted to say 'the real thing') Our motto is: 'If at first you do succeed, quit trying.'"

"Let me add a few thoughts about your own investments. Most investors, both institutional and individual, will find that the best way to own common stocks is through an index fund that charges minimal fees. Those following this path are sure to beat the net results (after fees and expenses) delivered by the great majority of investment professionals. Should you choose, however, to construct your own portfolio, there are a few thoughts worth remembering. Intelligent investing is not complex, though that is far from saying that it is easy. What an investor needs is the ability to correctly evaluate selected businesses. Note that word 'selected': You don't have to be an expert on every company, or even many. You only have to be able to evaluate companies within your circle of competence. The size of that circle is not very important; knowing its boundaries, however, is vital. To invest successfully, you need not understand beta, efficient markets, modern portfolio theory, option pricing or emerging markets. You may, in fact, be better off knowing nothing of these. That, of course, is not the prevailing view at most business schools, whose finance curriculum tends to be dominated by such subjects. In our view, though, investment students need only two well-taught courses – How to Value a Business, and How to Think About Market Prices. Your goal as an investor should simply be to purchase, at a rational price, a part interest in an easily-understandable business whose earnings are virtually certain to be materially higher five, ten and twenty years from now. Over time, you will find only a few companies that meet these standards – so when you see one that qualifies, you should buy a meaningful amount of stock. You must also resist the temptation to stray from your guidelines: If you aren't willing to own a stock for ten years, don't even think about owning it for ten minutes. Put together a portfolio of companies whose aggregate earnings march upward over the years, and so also will the portfolio's market value. Though it's seldom recognized, this is the exact approach that has produced gains for Berkshire shareholders: Our look-through earnings have grown at a good clip over the years, and our stock price has risen correspondingly. Had those gains in earnings not materialized, there would have been little increase in Berkshire's value."

"If you really analyze businesses, so you are buying into a business and making a conscious decision about what you think the future of that business is, I really think that if you can find six or eight [companies], then that's plenty."

Benjamin Graham

"I read the first edition of this book [The Intelligent Investor by Benjamin Graham] early in 1950, when I was nineteen. I thought it was by far the best book about investing ever written. I still think it is."

"To invest successfully over a lifetime does not require a stratospheric IQ, unusual business insights, or inside information. What's needed is a sound intellectual framework for making decisions and the ability to keep emotions from corroding that framework. This book [The Intelligent Investor by Benjamin Graham] precisely and clearly prescribes the proper framework. You must supply the emotional discipline."

"That book [The Intelligent Investor] was my Ten Commandments. It gave me the framework for thinking about business and investments and I haven't changed it."

"To me, Ben Graham was far more than an author or a teacher. More than any other man except my father, he influenced my life."

"A bit of nostalgia: It was exactly 50 years ago that I entered Ben Graham's class at Columbia. During the decade before, I had enjoyed – make that loved – analyzing, buying, and selling stocks. But my results were no better than average. Beginning in 1951 my performance improved. No, I hadn't changed my diet or taken up exercise. The only new ingredient was Ben's ideas. Quite simply, a few hours spent at the feet of the master proved far more valuable to me than had ten years of supposedly original thinking. In addition to being a great teacher, Ben was a wonderful friend. My debt to him is incalculable."

"This is the 100th anniversary of Ben's birth, I believe. And on the creative side, if what I consider his three basic ideas are really ground into your intellectual framework, I don't see how you can help but do reasonably well in stocks. His three basic ideas – and none of them are complicated or require any mathematical talent or anything of the sort – are that you should look at stocks as part ownership of a business, that you should look at market fluctuations in terms of his 'Mr Market' example and make them your friend rather than your enemy by essentially profiting from folly rather than participating in it, and finally, the three most important words in investing are 'margin of safety' – which Ben talked about in his last chapter of The Intelligent Investor – always building a 15,000 pound bridge if you're going to be driving 10,000 pound trucks across it. I think those three ideas 100 years from now will still be regarded as the three cornerstones, essentially, of sound investment. And that's what Ben was all about. He wasn't about brilliant investing. He wasn't about fads or fashion. He was about sound investing. And what's nice is that sound investing can make you very wealthy if you're not in too big a hurry. And it never makes you poor – which is even better. So I think that it comes down to those ideas – although they sound so simple and commonplace that it kind of seems like a waste to go to school and get a PH.D. in Economics and

have it all come back to that. It's a little like spending
eight years in divinity school and having somebody tell
you that the ten commandments were all that counted.
There is a certain natural tendency to overlook
anything that simple and important. But those are the
important ideas. And they will still be the important
ideas 100 years from now. And we will owe them
to Ben."

Berkshire Hathaway

"In a sense, Berkshire Hathaway is a canvas, and I get to paint anything I want on that canvas. And it's the process of painting that I really enjoy, not selling the painting."

"Berkshire Hathaway is my canvas, and I think I'm working on the Sistine Chapel."

"There's nothing in my religious upbringing that causes me to recoil from stock splits. I'm on the boards of three companies, two of which have split their stock in the last couple of years. I happen to think that by not splitting Berkshire stock, we attract a slightly more long-term oriented group of investors. What you want to do is attract shareholders that are very much like you, with the same time horizons and expectations. We don't talk about quarterly earnings, we don't have an investor relations department, and we don't have conference calls with Wall Street Analysts, because we don't want people who are focusing on what's going to happen next quarter or even next year. We want people to join us because they want to be with us until they die."

"Were we to split the stock or take other actions focusing on stock price rather than business value, we would attract an entering class of buyers inferior to the exiting class of sellers. At $1300, there are very few investors who can't afford a Berkshire share. Would a potential one-share purchaser be better off if we split 100 for 1 so he could buy 100 shares? Those who think so and who would buy the stock because of the split or in anticipation of one would definitely downgrade the quality of our present shareholder group. (Could we really improve our shareholder group by trading some of our present clear-thinking members for impressionable new ones who, preferring paper to value, feel wealthier with nine $10 bills than with one $100 bill?) People who buy for non-value reasons are likely to sell for non-value reasons. Their presence in the picture will accentuate erratic price swings unrelated to underlying business developments." (Said in 1983)

"Not splitting the stock means to some extent I filter out people who think that a stock split is a wonderful thing. It doesn't have anything to do with the value of the business, like having a pizza that's cut into eight pieces instead of four pieces."

"I once had a friend who had a 60th birthday party. I couldn't make it to the party, so I sent him a card saying I wish he'd live until Berkshire stock splits. I still wish him the same."

"We will not repurchase shares unless we believe Berkshire stock is selling well below intrinsic value, conservatively calculated. Nor will we attempt to talk the stock up or down. (Neither publicly or privately have I ever told anyone to buy or sell Berkshire shares). Instead we will give all shareholders – and potential shareholders – the same valuation-related information we would wish to have if our positions were reversed."

"In terms of not paying dividends, we don't pay dividends because we think we can turn every dollar we make into more than a dollar in market value. The only reason for us to keep your money is to make it worth more by us keeping it than it would be worth if we gave it to you. That's the test, if we come to the conclusion that we can't do that, we should distribute it to you. The interesting thing is we have certain businesses, See's Candy being one, where we don't have a way to intelligently use all of the money that See's generates within See's candy company. So if See's were a stand-alone company, it would pay very large dividends, not because it had a dividend paying policy, but because it wouldn't have a way of using, in this case, $30 million a year in intelligently expanding that business. We hope that in the overall Berkshire Hathaway scheme of things, that we can intelligently use the money that the companies in aggregate generate for us and we think so far we have, and we think the prospects are reasonably good that we can continue to do that. But dividend policy should really be determined by that criteria, also keeping in mind the possibilities of repurchasing stock."

"One usage of retained earnings we often greet with special enthusiasm when practiced by companies in which we have an investment interest is repurchase of their own shares. The reasoning is simple: if a fine business is selling in the market place for far less than intrinsic value, what more certain or more profitable utilization of capital can there be than significant enlargement of the interests of all owners at that bargain price? The competitive nature of corporate acquisition activity almost guarantees the payment of a full – frequently more than full – price when a company buys the entire ownership of another enterprise. But the auction nature of security markets often allows finely-run companies the opportunity to purchase portions of their own businesses at a price under 50% of that needed to acquire the same earning power through the negotiated acquisition of another enterprise."

"We generally like the policy of companies that have really wonderful businesses repurchasing their shares. The problem with most companies repurchasing their shares is that they are frequently so-so businesses and they are repurchasing shares for purposes other than intensifying the interest of shareholders in a wonderful business."

"I find it uncomfortable when friends or acquaintances mention that they are buying X because it has been reported – incorrectly – that Berkshire is a buyer. However, I do not set them straight. If they want to participate in whatever Berkshire actually is buying, they can always purchase Berkshire stock. But perhaps that is too simple. Usually, I suspect, they find it more exciting to buy what is being talked about. Whether that strategy is more profitable is another question."

"I've warned you in the past that you should not believe everything you read or hear about Berkshire – even when it is published or broadcast by a prestigious news organization."

"Through our policies and communications - our 'advertisements' - we try to attract investors who will understand our operations, attitudes and expectations. (And, fully as important, we try to dissuade those who won't). We want those who think of themselves as business owners and invest in companies with the intention of staying a long time. And, we want those who keep their eyes focused on business results, not market prices."

"We try to communicate in a way that turns people off who have a crazy approach to stocks. It matters as much who you repel as who you attract. If we were sizably owned by day traders, we'd have crazy valuations in no time - and in both directions."

"We will try to avoid policies that attract buyers with a short-term focus on our stock price and try to follow policies that attract informed long-term investors focusing on business values."

"In the end, Charlie and I do not care whether our shareholders own Berkshire in large or small amounts. What we wish for are shareholders of any size who are knowledgeable about our operations, share our objectives and long-term perspective, and are aware of our limitations, most particularly those imposed by our large capital base."

"You should be fully aware of one attitude Charlie and I share that hurts our financial performance: Regardless of price, we have no interest at all in selling any good businesses that Berkshire owns. We are also very reluctant to sell sub-par businesses as long as we expect them to generate at least some cash and as long as we feel good about their managers and labor relations. We hope not to repeat the capital-allocation mistakes that led us into such sub-par businesses. And we react with great caution to suggestions that our poor businesses can be restored to satisfactory profitability by major capital expenditures. (The projections will be dazzling and the advocates sincere, but, in the end, major additional investment in a terrible industry usually is about as rewarding as struggling in quicksand). Nevertheless, gin rummy managerial behavior (discard your least promising business at each turn) is not our style. We would rather have our overall results penalized a bit than engage in that kind of behavior."

"We wish for very little trading activity. If we ran a private business with a few passive partners, we would be disappointed if those partners, and their replacements, frequently wanted to leave the partnership. Running a public company, we feel the same way. Our goal is to attract long-term owners, who, at the time of purchase, have no timetable or price target for sale but plan instead to stay with us indefinitely. We don't understand the CEO who wants lots of stock activity, for that can be achieved only if many of his owners are constantly exiting. At what other organization - school, club, church, etc. - do leaders cheer when members leave? (However, if there were a broker whose livelihood depended upon the membership turnover in such organizations, you could be sure that there would be at least one proponent of activity, as in: 'There hasn't been much going on in Christianity for a while; maybe we should switch to Buddhism next week')."

"In effect, our shareholders behave in respect to their Berkshire stock much as Berkshire itself behaves in respect to companies in which it has an investment. As owners of, say, Coca-Cola or Gillette shares, we think of Berkshire as being a non-managing partner in two extraordinary businesses, in which we measure our success by the long-term progress of the companies rather than by the month-to-month movements of their stocks. In fact, we would not care in the least if several years went by in which there was no trading, or quotation of prices, in the stocks of those companies. If we have good long term expectations, short-term price changes are meaningless for us except to the extent they offer us an opportunity to increase our ownership at an attractive price."

"At Berkshire, we make no attempt to pick the few winners that will emerge from an ocean of unproven enterprises. We're not smart enough to do that, and we know it. Instead, we try to apply Aesop's 2,600-year-old equation to opportunities in which we have reasonable confidence as to how many birds are in the bush and when they will emerge (a formulation that my grandsons would probably update to 'A girl in a convertible is worth five in the phonebook'). Obviously, we can never precisely predict the timing of cash flows in and out of a business or their exact amount. We try, therefore, to keep our estimates conservative and to focus on industries where business surprises are unlikely to wreak havoc on owners. Even so, we make many mistakes: I'm the fellow, remember, who thought he understood the future economics of trading stamps, textiles, shoes and second-tier department stores."

"Our holdings of Coca-Cola increased from 14,172,500 shares at the end of 1988 to 23,350,000. This Coca-Cola investment provides yet another example of the incredible speed with which your Chairman responds to investment opportunities, no matter how obscure or well-disguised they may be. I believe I had my first Coca-Cola in either 1935 or 1936. Of a certainty, it was in 1936 that I started buying Cokes at the rate of six for 25¢ from Buffett & Son, the family grocery store, to sell around the neighborhood for 5¢ each. In this excursion into high-margin retailing, I duly observed the extraordinary consumer attractiveness and commercial possibilities of the product. I continued to note these qualities for the next 52 years as Coke blanketed the world. During this period, however, I carefully avoided buying even a single share, instead allocating major portions of my net worth to street railway companies, windmill manufacturers, anthracite producers, textile businesses, trading-stamp issuers, and the like. (If you think I'm making this up, I can supply the names). Only in the summer of 1988 did my brain finally establish contact with my eyes."

"Let me add a lesson from history: Coke went public in 1919 at $40 per share. By the end of 1920 the market, coldly reevaluating Coke's future prospects, had battered the stock down by more than 50%, to $19.50. At yearend 1993, that single share, with dividends reinvested, was worth more than $2.1 million. As Ben Graham said: 'In the short-run, the market is a voting machine – reflecting a voter-registration test that requires only money, not intelligence or emotional stability – but in the long-run, the market is a weighing machine.'"

"In 1938, more than 50 years after the introduction of Coke, and long after the drink was firmly established as an American Icon, Fortune did an excellent story on the company. In the second paragraph the writer reported: 'Several times every year a weighty and serious investor looks long and with profound respect at Coca-Cola's record, but comes regretfully to the conclusion that he is looking too late. The specters of saturation and competition rise before him.' Yes, competition there was in 1938 and in 1993 as well. But it's worth noting that in 1938 The Coca-Cola Co. sold 207 million cases of soft drinks (if its gallonage then is converted into the 192-ounce cases used for measurement today) and in 1993 it sold about 10.7 billion cases, a 50-fold increase in physical volume from a company that in 1938 was already dominant in its very major industry. Nor was the party over in 1938 for an investor: Though the $40 invested in 1919 in one share had (with dividends reinvested) turned into $3,277 by the end of 1938, a fresh $40 then invested in Coca-Cola stock would have grown to $25,000 by yearend 1993. I can't resist one more quote from that 1938 Fortune story: 'It would be hard to name any company comparable in size to Coca-Cola and selling, as Coca-Cola does, an unchanged product that can point to a ten-year record anything like Coca-Cola's.' In the 55 years that have since passed, Coke's product line has broadened somewhat, but it's remarkable how well that description still fits."

"Debt is a four-letter word around Berkshire."

"We use debt sparingly and, when we do borrow, we attempt to structure our loans on a long-term fixed-rate basis. We will reject interesting opportunities rather than over-leverage our balance sheet. This conservatism has penalized our results but it is the only behavior that leaves us comfortable, considering our fiduciary obligations to policyholders, lenders and the many equity holders who have committed unusually large portions of their net worth to our care. (As one of the Indianapolis '500' winners said: 'To finish first, you must first finish')."

"We cherish cost-consciousness at Berkshire. Our model is the widow who went to the local newspaper to place an obituary notice. Told there was a 25-cents-a-word charge, she requested 'Fred Brown died.' She was then informed there was a seven-word minimum. 'Okay' the bereaved woman replied, make it 'Fred Brown died, golf clubs for sale.'"

"We neither understand the adding of unneeded people or activities because profits are booming, nor the cutting of essential people or activities because profitability is shrinking. That kind of yo-yo approach is neither business-like nor humane. Our goal is to do what makes sense for Berkshire's customers and employees at all times, and never add to the unneeded."

"Our financial growth has been matched by employment growth: We now have 47,566 on our payroll, with the acquisitions of 1998 bringing 7,074 employees to us and internal growth adding another 2,500. To balance this gain of 9,500 in hands-on employees, we have enlarged the staff at world headquarters from 12 to 12.8. (The .8 doesn't refer to me or Charlie: We have a new person in accounting, working four days a week.) Despite this alarming trend toward corporate bloat, our after-tax overhead last year was about $3.5 million, or well under one basis point (.01 of 1%) of the value of the assets we manage."

"A compact organization lets all of us spend our time managing the business rather than managing each other."

"At Berkshire, we believe in Charlie's dictum – 'Just tell me the bad news; the good news will take care of itself' – and that is the behavior we expect of our managers when they are reporting to us."

"At Berkshire, we have no view of the future that dictates what businesses or industries we will enter. Indeed, we think it's usually poison for a corporate giant's shareholders if it embarks upon new ventures pursuant to some grand vision. We prefer instead to focus on the economic characteristics of businesses that we wish to own and the personal characteristics of managers with whom we wish to associate – and then to hope we get lucky in finding the two in combination."

"We will continue to follow our familiar formula, striving to increase the value of the excellent businesses we have, adding new businesses of similar quality, and issuing shares only grudgingly."

"Our Website, like our name, annual report, and headquarters is meant to convey just what we are, a different sort of company. We are intentionally plain, like a woman who wears no makeup because it fits our personality and attitude."

"At Berkshire we feel that telling outstanding CEOs, such as Tony [Tony Nicely, CEO of Berkshire subsidiary GEICO], how to run their companies would be the height of foolishness. Most of our managers wouldn't work for us if they got a lot of backseat driving. (Generally, they don't have to work for anyone, since 75% or so are independently wealthy). Besides, they are the Mark McGwires of the business world and need no advice from us as to how to hold the bat or when to swing. Nevertheless, Berkshire's ownership may make even the best of managers more effective. First, we eliminate all of the ritualistic and nonproductive activities that normally go with the job of CEO. Our managers are totally in charge of their personal schedules. Second, we give each a simple mission: Just run your business as if 1) you own 100% of it; 2) it is the only asset in the world that you and your family have or will ever have; and 3) you can't sell or merge it for at least a century. As a corollary, we tell them they should not let any of their decisions be affected even slightly by accounting considerations. We want our managers to think about what counts, not how it will be counted.

Very few CEOs of public companies operate under a similar mandate, mainly because they have owners who focus on short-term prospects and reported earnings. Berkshire, however, has a shareholder base – which it will have for decades to come – that has the longest investment horizon to be found in the public-company universe. Indeed, a majority of our shares are held by investors who expect to die still holding them. We can therefore ask our CEOs to manage for maximum long-term value, rather than for next quarter's earnings. We certainly don't ignore the current results of our businesses – in most cases, they are of great importance – but we never want them to be achieved at the expense of our building ever-greater competitive strengths. I believe the GEICO story demonstrates the benefits of Berkshire's approach. Charlie and I haven't taught Tony a thing – and never will – but we have created an environment that allows him to apply all of his talents to what's important. He does not have to devote his time or energy to board meetings, press interviews, presentations by investment bankers or talks with financial analysts. Furthermore, he need never spend a moment thinking about financing, credit ratings or 'Street' expectations for earnings per share. Because of our ownership structure, he also knows that this operational framework will endure for decades to come. In this environment of freedom, both Tony and his company can convert their almost limitless potential into matching achievements."

"In 38 years, we've never had a single CEO of a subsidiary elect to leave Berkshire to work elsewhere."

"Whatever the future holds, I make you one promise: I'll keep at least 99% of my net worth in Berkshire for as long as I am around. How long will that be? My model is the loyal Democrat in Fort Wayne who asked to be buried in Chicago so that he could stay active in the party. To that end, I've already selected a 'power spot' at the office for my urn."

"In line with Berkshire's owner-orientation, most of our directors have a major portion of their net worth invested in the company. We eat our own cooking. Charlie's family has 90% or more of its net worth in Berkshire shares; my wife, Susie, and I have more than 99%. In addition, many of my relatives – my sisters and cousins, for example – keep a huge portion of their net worth in Berkshire stock. Charlie and I feel totally comfortable with this eggs-in-one-basket situation because Berkshire itself owns a wide variety of truly extraordinary businesses. Indeed, we believe that Berkshire is close to being unique in the quality and diversity of the businesses in which it owns either a controlling interest or a minority interest of significance. Charlie and I cannot promise you results. But we can guarantee that your financial fortunes will move in lockstep with ours for whatever period of time you elect to be our partner. We have no interest in large salaries or options or other means of gaining an 'edge' over you. We want to make money only when our partners do and in exactly the same proportion. Moreover, when I do something dumb, I want you to be able to derive some solace from the fact that my financial suffering is proportional to yours."

"If you're talking about just pure bread-and-butter equities, I like to buy something that I feel is so good in terms of the business they're in and the management and I feel so good about the price I bought in, then I say to myself 'I'd just as soon own this forever.' That's the way I want people to feel about Berkshire. I'm going to own Berkshire forever. I've never sold a share and I think you find a higher percentage of the people that own Berkshire say that they have no intention ever of selling it than just about any company and those are the kind of partners I want."

"Charlie and I hope that you do not think of yourself as merely owning a piece of paper whose price wiggles around daily and that is a candidate for sale when some economic or political event makes you nervous. We hope you instead visualize yourself as a part owner of a business that you expect to stay with indefinitely, much as you might if you owned a farm or apartment house in partnership with members of your family. For our part, we do not view Berkshire shareholders as faceless members of an ever-shifting crowd, but rather as co-venturers who have entrusted their funds to us for what may well turn out to be the remainder of their lives."

Management
and the Business

"We've read management treatises that specify exactly how many people should report to any one executive, but they make little sense to us. When you have able managers of high character running businesses about which they are passionate, you can have a dozen or more reporting to you and still have time for an afternoon nap. Conversely, if you have even one person reporting to you who is deceitful, inept or uninterested, you will find yourself with more than you can handle."

"Charlie and I know that the right players will make almost any team manager look good. We subscribe to the philosophy of Ogilvy & Mather's founding genius, David Ogilvy: 'If each of us hires people who are smaller than we are, we shall become a company of dwarfs. But, if each of us hires people who are bigger than we are, we shall become a company of giants.'"

"Our managers have produced extraordinary results by doing rather ordinary things – but doing them exceptionally well. Our managers protect their franchises, they control costs, they search for new products and markets that build on their existing strengths and they don't get diverted. They work exceptionally hard at the details of their businesses, and it shows."

"I learned to go into business only with people whom I like, trust, and admire. As I noted before, this policy of itself will not ensure success: A second-class textile or department-store company won't prosper simply because its managers are men that you would be pleased to see your daughter marry. However, an owner – or investor – can accomplish wonders if he manages to associate himself with such people in businesses that possess decent economic characteristics. Conversely, we do not wish to join with managers who lack admirable qualities, no matter how attractive the prospects of their business. We've never succeeded in making a good deal with a bad person."

"I have turned down business deals that were otherwise decent deals because I didn't like the people I would have to work with. I didn't see any sense in pretending. To get involved with people who cause your stomach to churn – I say it's a lot like marrying for money. It's probably a bad idea under any circumstances, but it's absolutely crazy if you're already rich."

"Whenever I read about some company undertaking a cost-cutting program, I know it's not a company that really knows what costs are all about. Spurts don't work in this area. The really good manager does not wake up in the morning and say, 'This is the day I'm going to cut costs,' anymore than he wakes up and decides to practice breathing."

"Our experience has been that the manager of an already high-cost operation frequently is uncommonly resourceful in finding new ways to add overhead, while the manager of a tightly run operation usually continues to find additional methods to curtail costs, even when his costs are already well below those of his competitors."

"I'm a better businessman because I am an investor and a better investor because I am a businessman. If you have the mentality of both, it aids you in each field."

"My conclusion from my own experiences and from much observation of other businesses is that a good managerial record (measured by economic returns) is far more a function of what business boat you get into than it is of how effectively you row (though intelligence and effort help considerably, of course, in any business, good or bad). Some years ago I wrote: 'When a management with a reputation for brilliance tackles a business with a reputation for poor fundamental economics, it is the reputation of the business that remains intact.' Nothing has changed my point of view on that matter. Should you find yourself in a chronically-leaking boat, energy devoted to changing vessels is likely to be more productive than energy devoted to patching leaks."

"Good jockeys will do well on good horses, but not on broken down nags."

"Both our operating and investment experience cause us to conclude that 'turn-arounds' seldom turn, and that the same energies and talent are much better employed in a good business purchased at a fair price than in a poor business purchased at a bargain price."

"Our Vice Chairman, Charlie Munger, has always emphasized the study of mistakes rather than successes, both in business and other aspects of life. He does so in the spirit of the man who said: 'All I want to know is where I'm going to die so I'll never go there.' You'll immediately see why we make a good team: Charlie likes to study errors and I have generated ample material for him, particularly in our textile and insurance businesses."

"We do not, however, see this long-term focus as eliminating the need for us to achieve decent short-term results as well. After all, we were thinking long-range thoughts five or ten years ago, and the moves we made then should now be paying off. If plantings made confidently are repeatedly followed by disappointing harvests, something is wrong with the farmer. (Or perhaps with the farm: Investors should understand that for certain companies, and even for some industries, there simply is no good long-term strategy. Just as you should be suspicious of managers who pump up short-term earnings by accounting maneuvers, asset sales and the like, so also should you be suspicious of those managers who fail to deliver for extended periods and blame it on their long-term focus. Even Alice, after listening to the Queen lecture her about 'jam tomorrow', finally insisted, 'It must come sometimes to jam today')."

"A cumulation of small managerial stupidities will produce a major stupidity – not a major triumph. (Las Vegas has been built upon the wealth transfers that occur when people engage in seemingly small disadvantageous capital transactions)."

"What should you be doing in running your business? Just what you always do: Widen the moat, build enduring competitive advantage, delight your customers, and relentlessly fight costs."

"The moat is what it's all about. If you can enlarge the moat and protect the business, everything else follows."

"Ben Graham taught me 45 years ago that in investing it is not necessary to do extraordinary things to get extraordinary results. In later life, I have been surprised to find that this statement holds true in business management as well. What a manager must do is handle the basics well and not get diverted."

"A far more serious problem occurs when the management of a great company gets sidetracked and neglects its wonderful base business while purchasing other businesses that are so-so or worse. When that happens, the suffering of investors is often prolonged. Unfortunately, that is precisely what transpired years ago at both Coke and Gillete. (Would you believe that a few decades back they were growing shrimp at Coke and exploring for oil at Gillette?) Loss of focus is what most worries Charlie and me when we contemplate investing in businesses that in general look outstanding. All too often, we've seen value stagnate in the presence of hubris or of boredom that caused the attention of managers to wander."

"Inevitably, of course, business errors will occur and the wise manager will try to find the proper lessons in them. But the trick is to learn most lessons from the experiences of others. Managers who have learned much from personal experience in the past usually are destined to learn much from personal experience in the future."

"Somebody once said that in looking for people to hire, you look for three qualities: integrity, intelligence, and energy. And if they don't have the first, the other two will kill you. You think about it, it's true. If you hire somebody without the first, you really want them to be dumb and lazy."

"I look for people with fire in their belly, people with passion, not what their grades are or where their degree is from. I look for intellect, energy and integrity."

"Good managers are so scarce I can't afford the luxury of letting them go just because they've added a year to their age."

"We do not remove superstars from our line-up merely because they have attained a specified age – whether the traditional 65, or the 95 reached by Mrs. B on the eve of Hanukkah in 1988. Superb managers are too scarce a resource to be discarded simply because a cake gets crowded with candles. Moreover, our experience with newly-minted MBAs has not been that great. Their academic records always look terrific and the candidates always know just what to say; but too often they are short on personal commitment to the company and general business savvy. It's difficult to teach a new dog old tricks."

Corporate Conduct

"If we are to disappoint you, we would rather it be with our earnings than with our accounting."

"In the long run, managements stressing accounting appearance over economic substance usually achieve little of either."

"Lately, those who have traveled the high road in Wall Street have not encountered heavy traffic."

"There is a crisis of confidence today about corporate earnings and the credibility of chief executives. And it's justified."

"For many years, I've had little confidence in the earnings numbers reported by most corporations. I'm not talking about Enron and Worldcom – examples of outright crookedness. Rather, I am referring to the legal, but improper, accounting methods used by chief executives to inflate reported earnings. The most flagrant deceptions have occurred in stock-option accounting and in assumptions about pension-fund returns. The aggregate misrepresentation in these two areas dwarfs the lies of Enron and Worldcom."

"Recently, a few CEOs have stepped forward to adopt honest accounting. But most continue to spend their shareholders' money, directly or through trade associations, to lobby against real reform. They talk principle, but, for most, their motive is pocketbook. For their shareholder's interest, and for the country's, CEOs should tell their accounting departments today to quit recording illusory pension-fund income and start recording all compensation costs. They don't need studies or new rules to do that. They just need to act."

"At Berkshire you will find no 'big bath' accounting maneuvers or restructurings nor any 'smoothing' of quarterly or annual results. We will always tell you how many strokes we have taken on each hole and never play around with the scoreboard. When the numbers are a very rough 'guess estimate,' as they necessarily must be in insurance reserving, we will try to be both consistent and conservative in our approach."

"I will keep well over 99% of my net worth in Berkshire. My wife and I have never sold a share nor do we intend to. Charlie and I are disgusted by the situation, so common in the last few years, in which shareholders have suffered billions in losses while the CEOs, promoters, and other higher-ups who fathered these disasters have walked away with extraordinary wealth. Indeed, many of these people were urging investors to buy shares while concurrently dumping their own, sometimes using methods that hid their actions. To their shame, these business leaders view shareholders as patsies, not partners."

"In 1961, President Kennedy said that we should ask not what our country can do for us, but rather ask what we can do for our country. Last year we decided to give his suggestion a try – and who says it never hurts to ask? We were told to mail $860 million in income taxes to the U.S. treasury. Here's a little perspective on that figure: If an equal amount had been paid by only 2,000 other taxpayers, the government would have had a balanced budget in 1996 without needing a dime of taxes – income or Social Security or what have you – from any other American. Berkshire shareholders can truly say, 'I gave at the office.' Charlie and I believe that large tax payments by Berkshire are entirely fitting. The contribution we thus make to society's well-being is at most only proportional to its contribution to ours. Berkshire prospers in America as it would nowhere else."

"In all of our communications, we try to make sure that no single shareholder gets an edge: We do not follow the usual practice of giving earnings 'guidance' or other information of value to analysts or large shareholders. Our goal is to have all of our owners updated at the same time."

"When you do receive a communication from us, it will come from the fellow you are paying to run the business. Your Chairman has a firm belief that owners are entitled to hear directly from the CEO as to what is going on and how he evaluates the business, currently and prospectively. You would demand that in a private company; you should expect no less in a public company. A once-a-year report of stewardship should not be turned over to a staff specialist or public relations consultant who is unlikely to be in a position to talk frankly on a manager-to-owner basis."

"At Berkshire, full reporting means giving you the information that we would wish you to give us if our positions were reversed. What Charlie and I would want under that circumstance would be all the important facts about current operations as well as the CEO's frank view of the long-term economic characteristics of the business. We would expect both a lot of financial details and a discussion of any significant data we would need to interpret what was presented. When Charlie and I read reports, we have no interest in pictures of personnel, plants or products. References to EBITDA [Earnings Before Interest, Taxes, Depreciation and Amortization] make us shudder – does management think the tooth fairy pays for capital expenditures? We're very suspicious of accounting methodology that is vague or unclear, since too often that means management wishes to hide something. And we don't want to read messages that a public relations department or consultant has turned out. Instead, we expect a company's CEO to explain in his or her own words what's happening."

"Three suggestions for investors: First, beware of companies displaying weak accounting. If a company still does not expense options, or if its pension assumptions are fanciful, watch out. When managements take the low road in aspects that are visible, it is likely they are following a similar path behind the scenes. There is seldom just one cockroach in the kitchen. Trumpeting EBITDA (Earnings Before Interest, Taxes, Depreciation and Amortization) is a particularly pernicious practice...Second, unintelligible footnotes usually indicate untrustworthy management. If you can't understand a footnote or other managerial explanation, it's usually because the CEO doesn't want you to. Enron's descriptions of certain transactions still baffle me. Finally, be suspicious of companies that trumpet earnings projections and growth expectations. Businesses seldom operate in a tranquil, no-surprise environment, and earnings simply don't advance smoothly (except, of course, in the offering books of investment bankers). Charlie and I not only don't know today what our businesses will earn next year – we don't even know what they will earn next quarter. We are suspicious of those CEOs who regularly claim they do know the future – and we become downright incredulous if they consistently reach their declared targets. Managers that always promise to 'make the numbers' will at some point be tempted to make up the numbers."

"Clearly the attitude of disrespect that many executives have today for accurate reporting is a business disgrace. And auditors, as we have suggested, have done little on the positive side. Though auditors should regard the investing public as their client, they tend to kowtow instead to the managers who choose them and dole out their pay ('Whose bread I eat, his song I sing')."

"Enron is grotesque in what happened, but there's no question that auditors have been unduly compliant in past years. They approved quite dubious accounting, they weren't working for shareholders – they were working for management."

"In recent years, probity has eroded. Many major corporations still play things straight, but a significant and growing number of otherwise high-grade managers – CEOs you would be happy to have as spouses for your children or as trustees under your will – have come to the view that it's okay to manipulate earnings to satisfy what they believe are Wall Street's desires. Indeed, many CEOs think this kind of manipulation is not only okay, but actually their duty. These managers start with the assumption, all too common, that their job at all times is to encourage the highest stock price possible (a premise with which we adamantly disagree). To pump the price, they strive, admirably, for operational excellence. But when operations don't produce the result hoped for, these CEOs resort to unadmirable accounting stratagems. These either manufacture the desired 'earnings' or set the stage for them in the future. Rationalizing this behavior, these managers often say that their shareholders will be hurt if their currency for doing deals – that is, their stock – is not fully-priced, and they also argue that in using accounting shenanigans to get the figures they want, they are only doing what everybody else does. Once such an everybody's-doing-it attitude takes hold, ethical misgivings vanish. Call this behavior Son of Gresham: Bad accounting drives out good."

"One further thought while I'm on my soapbox: Charlie and I think it is both deceptive and dangerous for CEOs to predict growth rates for their companies. They are, of course, frequently egged on to do so by both analysts and their own investor relations departments. They should resist, however, because too often these predictions lead to trouble. It's fine for a CEO to have his own internal goals and, in our view, it's even appropriate for the CEO to publicly express some hopes about the future, if these expectations are accompanied by sensible caveats. But for a major corporation to predict that its per-share earnings will grow over the long term at, say, 15% annually is to court trouble. That's true because a growth rate of that magnitude can only be maintained by a very small percentage of large businesses. Here's a test: Examine the record of, say, the 200 highest earning companies from 1970 or 1980 and tabulate how many have increased per-share earnings by 15% annually since those dates. You will find that only a handful have. I would wager you a very significant sum that fewer than 10 of the 200 most profitable companies in 2000 will attain 15% annual growth in earnings-per-share over the next 20 years."

"The problem arising from lofty predictions is not just that they spread unwarranted optimism. Even more troublesome is the fact that they corrode CEO behavior. Over the years, Charlie and I have observed many instances in which CEOs engaged in uneconomic operating maneuvers so that they could meet earnings targets they had announced. Worse still, after exhausting all that operating acrobatics would do, they sometimes played a wide variety of accounting games to 'make the numbers.' These accounting shenanigans have a way of snowballing: Once a company moves earnings from one period to another, operating shortfalls that occur thereafter require it to engage in further accounting maneuvers that must be even more 'heroic.' These can turn fudging into fraud (More money, it has been noted, has been stolen with the point of a pen than at the point of a gun). Charlie and I tend to be leery of companies run by CEOs who woo investors with fancy predictions. A few of these managers will prove prophetic – but others will turn out to be congenital optimists, or even charlatans. Unfortunately, it's not easy for investors to know in advance which species they are dealing with."

"In reality, however, earnings can be as pliable as putty when a charlatan heads the company reporting them. Eventually truth will surface, but in the meantime a lot of money can change hands. Indeed, some important American fortunes have been created by the monetization of accounting mirages."

"We will be candid in our reporting to you, emphasizing the pluses and minuses important in appraising business value. Our guideline is to tell you the business facts that we would want to know if your positions were reversed. We owe you no less. Moreover, as a company with a major communications business, it would be inexcusable for us to apply lesser standards of accuracy, balance and incisiveness when reporting on ourselves than we would expect our news people to apply when reporting on others. We also believe candor benefits us as managers: The CEO who misleads others in public may eventually mislead himself in private."

"I would suggest some certain behavior for the CEO, and then I would suggest a way of possibly enforcing it. I would suggest that the CEO regard himself as the chief disclosure officer of a company, that he write his own letter. And, he can certainly call on an editor. I have the world's best editor, who is here today, Carol Loomis. And, it's enormously useful to have a wonderful editor. But the CEO should still write the letter. And the CEO should write that letter as if he had one partner, and that partner has been away for a year. The partner is intelligent. He's somewhat versed in accounting terminology and finance terminology, but he's no expert. He's interested because he has a large section of his net worth in the company. He's ready to be an indefinite shareholder – a shareholder for an indefinite period, if he's treated well. And the CEO, if he has that mental picture of that partner, and just writes to that partner what's happened that year, I think that's going to be better than all the information that can be required by any rules, because the CEO has a definite desire to communicate to that partner. And, I say the CEO's attitude should be what would I want, if our positions were reversed? It's that simple. I mean, what do I need to know? Now, Berkshire owns pieces of businesses – small pieces of businesses – and we own entire businesses. And, we really want the same disclosure from the CEOs of both companies. Not in the same detail, not something that could work to a competitive disadvantage, which if we own a hundred percent of a company, I'm perfectly willing to have him tell me about that, but I wouldn't want that done if I own five percent of a company. But in terms of the tone, the candor, I would want, from the CEO of a subsidiary of Berkshire, I would expect them to tell me what the hell is going on, and I would expect them to tell me that directly, and not have a public relations firm or an investor relations firm write the report for me. I don't want it coming to me with a lot of pictures or whatever it may be. I just want to know what's going on in their business. And, there's no reason why the CEO of a public company, leaving out some of the details, leaving out some competitive aspects – but there's no reason why the CEO can't talk to his owners the same way that a subsidiary manager of a Berkshire company talks to his owner, which is me."

"I really think that the disclosure problem does not revolve around the quantity of disclosure. I mean, the SEC and the auditing profession have provided us with just a wealth of information on a quantitative basis. But in the end, it's the CEO that determines the qualitative aspect of disclosure, and that's all important. And I think, under any rules, the CEO, if he or she wants to obfuscate, they can do that; and if they want to make it clear, they can do that. If they want to provide you with fluff, they can do that. If they want to provide you with substance, they can do that. The CEO will look at any rules through his own particular glasses, and either look at them as a way to give his shareholders more information, or to do some kind of tap dance number."

"Though Enron has become the symbol for shareholder abuse, there is no shortage of egregious conduct elsewhere in corporate America."

"We will always have people who misbehave in our midst and people will be attracted to large markets, but the presence of tough rules and tough cops, sure and swift prosecution is probably the best thing that can be done to minimize it."

"What we really deplore are the attempts by corporations to solve operating problems with accounting maneuvers. It catches up with you, sometimes with disastrous results. You might as well face reality immediately."

"There are indications that several large insurers opted in 1982 for obscure accounting and reserving maneuvers that masked significant deterioration in their underlying businesses. In insurance, as elsewhere, the reaction of weak managements to weak operations is often weak accounting ('It's difficult for an empty sack to stand upright')."

"In the long run, of course, trouble awaits managements that paper over operating problems with accounting maneuvers. Eventually, managements of this kind achieve the same result as the seriously-ill patient who tells his doctor: 'I can't afford the operation, but would you accept a small payment to touch up the x-rays?'"

Corporate Conduct

(Mergers & Acquisitions)

"In the acquisition arena, restructuring has been raised to art form: Managements now frequently use mergers to dishonestly rearrange the value of assets and liabilities in ways that will allow them to both smooth and swell future earnings. Indeed, at deal time, major auditing firms sometimes point out the possibilities for a little accounting magic (or for a lot). Getting this push from the pulpit, first-class people will frequently stoop to third-class tactics. CEOs understandably do not find it easy to reject auditor-blessed strategies that lead to increased future 'earnings.'"

"If we are to disappoint you, we would rather it be with our earnings than with our accounting. In all of our acquisitions, we have left the loss reserve figures exactly as we found them. After all, we have consistently joined with insurance managers knowledgeable about their business and honest in their financial reporting. When deals occur in which liabilities are increased immediately and substantially, simple logic says that at least one of those virtues must have been lacking – or, alternatively, that the acquirer is laying the groundwork for future infusions of 'earnings.'"

"The role that managements have played in stock-option accounting has hardly been benign: A distressing number of both CEOs and auditors have in recent years bitterly fought FASB's attempts to replace option fiction with truth and virtually none have spoken out in support of FASB [The Financial Accounting Standards Board]. Its opponents even enlisted Congress in the fight, pushing the case that inflated figures were in the national interest. Still I believe that the behavior of managements has been even worse when it comes to restructurings and merger accounting. Here, many managements purposefully work at manipulating numbers and deceiving investors. And, as Michael Kinsley has said about Washington: 'The scandal isn't in what's done that's illegal but rather in what's legal.'"

"I am very skeptical of most big mergers. The assumptions made tend to be very optimistic. People want to do deals – you start with that. There's a lot of Darwin going on in companies. And people who get to the top want action. I've been on 19 boards in my life, and I'd say the great majority of deals that I've seen were not very good deals."

"Agonizing over errors is a mistake. But acknowledging and analyzing them can be useful, though that practice is rare in corporate boardrooms. There, Charlie and I have almost never witnessed a candid post-mortem of a failed decision, particularly one involving an acquisition. A notable exception to this never-look-back approach is that of the Washington Post Company, which unfailingly and objectively reviews its acquisitions three years after they are made. Elsewhere, triumphs are trumpeted, but dumb decisions either get no follow-up or are rationalized. The financial consequences of these boners are regularly dumped into massive restructuring charges or write-offs that are casually waved off as 'nonrecurring.' Managements just love these. Indeed, in recent years it has seemed that no earnings statement is complete without them. The origins of these charges, though, are never explored. When it comes to corporate blunders, CEOs invoke the concept of the Virgin Birth."

"At other companies, executives may devote themselves to pursuing acquisition possibilities with investment bankers, utilizing an auction process that has become standardized. In this exercise the bankers prepare a 'book' that makes me think of the Superman comics of my youth. In the Wall Street version, a formerly mild-mannered company emerges from the investment banker's phone booth able to leap over competitors in a single bound and with earnings moving faster than a speeding bullet. Titillated by the book's description of the acquiree's powers, acquisition-hungry CEOs – Lois Lanes all, beneath their cool exteriors – promptly swoon. What's particularly entertaining in these books is the precision with which earnings are projected for many years ahead. If you ask the author-banker, however, what his own firm will earn next month, he will go into a protective crouch and tell you that business and markets are far too uncertain for him to venture a forecast."

"We believe most deals do damage to the shareholders of the acquiring company. Too often, the words from HMS Pinafore apply:'Things are seldom what they seem, skim milk masquerades as cream.' Specifically, sellers and their representatives invariably present financial projections having more entertainment value than educational value. In the production of rosy scenarios, Wall Street can hold its own against Washington. In any case, why potential buyers even look at projections prepared by sellers baffles me. Charlie and I never give them a glance, but instead keep in mind the story of the man with an ailing horse. Visiting the vet, he said: 'Can you help me? Sometimes my horse walks just fine and sometimes he limps.' The vet's reply was pointed: 'No problem – when he's walking fine, sell him.' In the world of mergers and acquisitions, that horse would be peddled as Secretariat."

"Charlie and I frequently get approached about acquisitions that don't come close to meeting our tests: We've found that if you advertise an interest in buying collies, a lot of people will call hoping to sell you their cocker spaniels. A line from a country song expresses our feeling about new ventures, turnarounds, or auction-like sales: 'When the phone don't ring, you'll know it's me.'"

"As we look at the major acquisitions that others made during 1982, our reaction is not envy, but relief that we were non-participants. For in many of these acquisitions, managerial intellect wilted in competition with managerial adrenalin. The thrill of the chase blinded the pursuers to the consequences of the catch. Pascal's observation seems apt: 'It has struck me that all men's misfortunes spring from the single cause that they are unable to stay quietly in one room.'"

"In some mergers there truly are major synergies – though oftentimes the acquirer pays too much to obtain them – but at other times the cost and revenue benefits that are projected prove illusory. Of one thing, however, be certain: If a CEO is enthused about a particularly foolish acquisition, both his internal staff and his outside advisors will come up with whatever projections are needed to justify his stance. Only in fairy tales are emperors told that they are naked."

"In most acquisitions, it's better to be the target than the acquirer. The acquirer pays for the fact that he gets to haul back to his cave the carcass of the conquered animal. I am suspicious of people who just keep acquiring almost by the week, though. If you look at the outstanding companies – say, a Microsoft or an Intel or a Wal-Mart – their growth overwhelmingly has been internal. Frequently, if some company is on a real acquisition binge, they feel they're using funny money, and it has certain aspects of a chain-letter game. Beyond that, I'd like to see a period where merged companies just run by themselves after a deal, rather than moving around the accounting and putting up big restructuring charges. I get suspicious when there's too much activity. I like to see organic growth."

"My most surprising discovery: the overwhelming importance in business of an unseen force that we might call 'the institutional imperative.' In business school, I was given no hint of the imperative's existence and I did not intuitively understand it when I entered the business world. I thought then that decent, intelligent, and experienced managers would automatically make rational business decisions. But I learned over time that isn't so. Instead, rationality frequently wilts when the institutional imperative comes into play. For example: (1) As if governed by Newton's First Law of Motion, an institution will resist any change in its current direction; (2) Just as work expands to fill available time, corporate projects or acquisitions will materialize to soak up available funds; (3) Any business craving of the leader, however foolish, will be quickly supported by detailed rate-of-return and strategic studies prepared by his troops; and (4) The behavior of peer companies, whether they are expanding, acquiring, setting executive compensation or whatever, will be mindlessly imitated."

Corporate Conduct

(Allocation of Capital)

"When we control a company we get to allocate capital, whereas we are likely to have little or nothing to say about this process with marketable holdings. This point can be important because the heads of many companies are not skilled in capital allocation. Their inadequacy is not surprising. Most bosses rise to the top because they have excelled in an area such as marketing, production, engineering, administration – or, sometimes, institutional politics. Once they become CEOs, they face new responsibilities. They now must make capital allocation decisions, a critical job that they may have never tackled and that is not easily mastered. To stretch the point, it's as if the final step for a highly-talented musician was not to perform at Carnegie Hall but, instead, to be named Chairman of the Federal Reserve. The lack of skill that many CEOs have at capital allocation is no small matter: After ten years on the job, a CEO whose company annually retains earnings equal to 10% of net worth will have been responsible for the deployment of more than 60% of all the capital at work in the business. CEOs who recognize their lack of capital-allocation skills (which not all do) will often try to compensate by turning to their staffs, management consultants, or investment bankers. Charlie and I have frequently observed the consequences of such 'help.' On balance, we feel it is more likely to accentuate the capital-allocation problem than to solve it."

"Over time, the skill with which a company's managers allocate capital has an enormous impact on the enterprise's value. Almost by definition, a really good business generates far more money (at least after its early years) than it can use internally. The company could, of course, distribute the money to shareholders by way of dividends or share repurchases. But often the CEO asks a strategic planning staff, consultants or investment bankers whether an acquisition or two might make sense. That's like asking your interior decorator whether you need a $50,000 rug. The acquisition problem is often compounded by a biological bias: Many CEOs attain their position in part because they possess an abundance of animal spirits and ego. If an executive is heavily endowed with these qualities – which, it should be acknowledged, sometimes have their advantages – they won't disappear when he reaches the top. When such a CEO is encouraged by his advisors to make deals, he responds much as would a teenage boy who is encouraged by his father to have a normal sex life. It's not a push he needs."

"Charlie and I have the easy jobs at Berkshire: We do very little except allocate capital. And, even then, we are not all that energetic. We have one excuse, though: In allocating capital, activity does not correlate with achievement. Indeed, in the fields of investments and acquisitions, frenetic behavior is often counterproductive."

"I've been deploying capital since I was 11 and am still doing it. There's no master plan, we just try to survey the whole financial field. We look for things we understand, with a durable business advantage and where the price is right."

CEOs & Directors

"The supreme irony of business management is that it is far easier for an inadequate CEO to keep his job than it is for an inadequate subordinate. If a secretary, say, is hired for a job that requires typing ability of at least 80 words a minute and turns out to be capable of only 50 words a minute, she will lose her job in no time. There is a logical standard for this job; performance is easily measured; and if you can't make the grade, you're out. Similarly, if new sales people fail to generate sufficient business quickly enough, they will be let go. Excuses will not be accepted as a substitute for orders. However, a CEO who doesn't perform is frequently carried indefinitely. One reason is that performance standards for his job seldom exist. When they do, they are often fuzzy or they may be waived or explained away, even when the performance shortfalls are major and repeated. At too many companies, the boss shoots the arrow of managerial performance and then hastily paints the bullseye around the spot where it lands."

"Yardsticks seldom are discarded while yielding favorable readings. But when results deteriorate, most managers favor disposition of the yardstick rather than disposition of the manager."

"I believe in establishing yardsticks prior to the act; retrospectively, almost anything can be made to look good in relation to something or other."

"Another important, but seldom recognized, distinction between the boss and the foot soldier is that the CEO has no immediate superior whose performance is itself getting measured. The sales manager who retains a bunch of lemons in his sales force will soon be in hot water himself. It is in his immediate self-interest to promptly weed out his hiring mistakes. Otherwise, he himself may be weeded out. An office manager who has hired inept secretaries faces the same imperative. But the CEO's boss is a Board of Directors that seldom measures itself and is infrequently held to account for substandard corporate performance. If the Board makes a mistake in hiring, and perpetuates that mistake, so what? Even if the company is taken over because of the mistake, the deal will probably bestow substantial benefits on the outgoing Board members (The bigger they are, the softer they fall). Finally, relations between the Board and the CEO are expected to be congenial. At board meetings, criticism of the CEO's performance is often viewed as the social equivalent of belching. No such inhibitions restrain the office manager from critically evaluating the substandard typist. These points should not be interpreted as a blanket condemnation of CEOs or Boards of Directors: Most are able and hard-working, and a number are truly outstanding. But the management failings that Charlie and I have seen make us thankful that we are linked with the managers of our three permanent holdings. They love their businesses, they think like owners, and they exude integrity and ability."

"Directors must get rid of a manager who is mediocre or worse, no matter how likeable he may be. Directors must react as did the chorus-girl bride of an 85-year-old multimillionaire when he asked whether she would love him if he lost his money. 'Of course,' the young beauty replied, 'I would miss you, but I would still love you.'"

"If able but greedy managers over-reach and try to dip too deeply into the shareholders' pockets, directors must slap their hands. Since I wrote that, over-reaching has become common but few hands have been slapped. Why have intelligent and decent directors failed so miserably? The answer lies not in inadequate laws – it's always been clear that directors are obligated to represent the interests of shareholders – but rather in what I'd call 'boardroom atmosphere.' It's almost impossible, for example, in a boardroom populated by well-mannered people, to raise the question of whether the CEO should be replaced. It's equally awkward to question a proposed acquisition that has been endorsed by the CEO, particularly when his inside staff and outside advisors are present and unanimously support his decision (They wouldn't be in the room if they didn't). Finally, when the compensation committee – armed, as always, with support from a high-paid consultant – reports on a megagrant of options to the CEO, it would be like belching at the dinner table for a director to suggest that the committee reconsider. These 'social' difficulties argue for outside directors regularly meeting without the CEO – a reform that is being instituted and that I enthusiastically endorse. I doubt, however, that most of the other new governance rules and recommendations will provide benefits commensurate with the monetary and other costs they impose."

"The current cry is for 'independent' directors. It is certainly true that it is desirable to have directors who think and speak independently – but they must also be business-savvy, interested and shareholder-oriented. In my 1993 commentary, those are the three qualities I described as essential. Over a span of 40 years, I have been on 19 public-company boards (excluding Berkshire's) and have interacted with perhaps 250 directors. Most of them were 'independent' as defined by today's rules. But the great majority of these directors lacked at least one of the three qualities I value. As a result, their contribution to shareholder well-being was minimal at best and, too often, negative. These people, decent and intelligent though they were, simply did not know enough about business and/or care enough about shareholders to question foolish acquisitions or egregious compensation. My own behavior, I must ruefully add, frequently fell short as well: Too often I was silent when management made proposals that I judged to be counter to the interests of shareholders. In those cases, collegiality trumped independence."

"The requisites for board membership should be business savvy, interest in the job, and owner-orientation. Too often, directors are selected simply because they are prominent or add diversity to the board. That practice is a mistake. Furthermore, mistakes in selecting directors are particularly serious because appointments are so hard to undo: The pleasant but vacuous director need never worry about job security."

"Getting rid of mediocre CEOs and eliminating over-reaching by the able ones requires action by owners – big owners. The logistics aren't that tough: The owner-ship of stock has grown increasingly concentrated in recent decades, and today it would be easy for institu-tional managers to exert their will on problem situations. Twenty, or even fewer, of the largest institutions, acting together, could effectively reform corporate governance at a given company, simply by withholding their votes for directors who were tolerating odious behavior. In my view, this kind of concerted action is the only way that corporate stewardship can be meaningfully improved."

"I think there's been a tendency, generally, throughout corporate America in terms of somewhat overreaching in compensation that's developed in the last 10 years, and I think the latter point could be addressed if institutional investors simply took a stronger stand about what they would approve in that arena. I mean, if you look at the percentage of the rewards that now go to management from a business succeeding vs. what goes to the owners, that has changed; that equation has changed in the last 15 years. And it won't revert to a more moderate situation unless owners do something about it, and the truth is the only owners that can do that are the big institutional owners."

"Give An Account Of Thy Stewardship"

"Both the ability and fidelity of managers have long needed monitoring. Indeed, nearly 2,000 years ago, Jesus Christ addressed this subject, speaking (Luke 16:2) approvingly of 'a certain rich man' who told his manager, 'Give an account of thy stewardship; for thou mayest no longer be steward.' Accountability and stewardship withered in the last decade, becoming qualities deemed of little importance by those caught up in the Great Bubble. As stock prices went up, the behavioral norms of managers went down. By the late '90s, as a result, CEOs who traveled the high road did not encounter heavy traffic. Most CEOs, it should be noted, are men and women you would be happy to have as trustees for your children's assets or as next-door neighbors. Too many of these people, however, have in recent years behaved badly at the office, fudging numbers and drawing obscene pay for mediocre business achievements. These otherwise decent people simply followed the career path of Mae West: 'I was Snow White but I drifted.'"

"To clean up their act on these fronts, CEOs don't need 'independent' directors, oversight committees or auditors absolutely free of conflicts of interest. They simply need to do what's right. As Alan Greenspan forcefully declared last week, the attitudes and actions of CEOs are what determine corporate conduct."

"The important thing is that we have the right view of ourselves. If we have the right view of ourselves, that will lead to deeds that will give the world the right view of us."

"Lose money for the firm and I will be understanding; lose a shred of reputation for the firm and I will be ruthless."

"CEOs want to be respected and believed. They will be - and should be - only when they deserve to be. They should quit talking about some bad apples and reflect instead on their own behavior."

"The job of CEOs is now to regain America's trust - and for the country's sake it is important that they do so. They will not succeed in this endeavor, however, by way of fatuous ads, meaningless policy statements, or structural changes of boards and committees. Instead, CEOs must embrace stewardship as a way of life and treat their owners as partners, not patsies. It's time for CEOs to walk the walk."

"The best advice on corporate governance is in Luke 16:2."

"It takes 20 years to build a reputation and five minutes to ruin it. If you think about that, you'll do things differently."

Options

"The most egregious case of let's-not-face-up-to-reality behavior by executives and accountants has occurred in the world of stock options."

"Options are a huge cost for many corporations and a huge benefit to executives. No wonder, then, that they have fought ferociously to avoid making a charge against their earnings. Without blushing, almost all CEOs have told their shareholders that options are cost-free. For these CEOs I have a proposition: Berkshire Hathaway will sell you insurance, carpeting or any of our other products in exchange for options identical to those you grant yourselves. It'll all be cash-free. But do you really think your corporation will not have incurred a cost when you hand over the options in exchange for the carpeting? Or do you really think that placing a value on the option is just too difficult to do, one of your other excuses for not expensing them? If these are the opinions you honestly hold, call me collect. We can do business."

"At GEICO [A Berkshire subsidiary], we are paying in a way that makes sense for both our owners and our managers. We distribute merit badges, not lottery tickets: In none of Berkshire's subsidiaries do we relate compensation to our stock price, which our associates cannot affect in any meaningful way. Instead, we tie bonuses to each unit's business performance, which is the direct product of the unit's people. When that performance is terrific - as it has been at GEICO - there is nothing Charlie and I enjoy more than writing a big check."

"The GEICO plan exemplifies Berkshire's incentive compensation principles: Goals should be (1) tailored to the economics of the specific operating business; (2) simple in character so that the degree to which they are being realized can be easily measured; and (3) directly related to the daily activities of plan participants. As a corollary, we shun 'lottery tickets' arrangements, such as options on Berkshire shares, whose ultimate value - which could range from zero to huge - is totally out of the control of the person whose behavior we would like to affect. In our view, a system that produces quixotic payoffs will not only be wasteful for owners but may actually discourage the focused behavior we value in managers."

"At Berkshire, however, we use an incentive-compensation system that rewards key managers for meeting targets in their own bailiwicks. If See's does well, that does not produce incentive compensation at the News – nor vice versa. Neither do we look at the price of Berkshire stock when we write bonus checks. We believe good unit performance should be rewarded whether Berkshire stock rises, falls, or stays even. Similarly, we think average performance should earn no special rewards even if our stock should soar."

"We tie all top executive compensation to the performance of what's under their control. We don't tie it to the price of Berkshire stock."

"The accounting profession and the SEC should be shamed by the fact that they have long let themselves be muscled by business executives on the option-accounting issue. Additionally, the lobbying that executives engage in may have an unfortunate by-product: In my opinion, the business elite risks losing its credibility on issues of significance to society - about which it may have much of value to say - when it advocates the incredible on issues of significance to itself." (Said in 1992)

"At Berkshire we frequently buy companies that awarded options to their employees - and then we do away with the option program."

"It seems to me that the realities of stock options can be summarized quite simply: If options aren't a form of compensation, what are they? If compensation isn't an expense, what is it? And, if expenses shouldn't go into the calculation of earnings, where in the world should they go?"

"In effect, accounting principles offer management a choice: Pay employees in one form and count the cost, or pay them in another form and ignore the cost. Small wonder then that the use of options has mushroomed."

"Companies tell their shareholders that options do more to attract, retain and motivate employees than does cash. I believe that's often true. These companies should keep issuing options. But they also should account for this expense just like any other."

"It took particular courage on your part, and that will be recognized and remembered. If I could show my appreciation by stepping up my book orders, I would. But you're already getting all of my business."
(From Warren Buffett letter to Amazon.com CEO Jeff Bezos regarding Bezos's decision to start accounting for stock options as an expense)

"The Senate itself is the major reason corporations have been able to duck option expensing. On May 3, 1994, the Senate, led by Senator Joseph Lieberman, pushed the Financial Accounting Standards Board and Arthur Levitt, then chairman of the S.E.C., into backing down from mandating that options be expensed. Mr. Levitt has said that he regrets this retreat more than any other move he made during his tenure as chairman. Unfortunately, current S.E.C. leadership seems uninterested in correcting this matter. I don't believe in Congress setting accounting rules. But the Senate opened the floodgates in 1994 to an anything-goes reporting system, and it should close them now. Rather than holding hearings and fulminating, why doesn't the Senate just free the standards board by rescinding its 1994 action."

"A number of senators, led by Carl Levin and John McCain, are now revisiting the subject of properly accounting for options. They believe that American businesses, large or small, can stand honest reporting, and that after Enron-Andersen, no less will do. I think it is normally unwise for Congress to meddle with accounting standards. In this case, though, Congress fathered an improper standard, and I cheer its return to the crime scene."

"With the Senate in its pocket and the SEC outgunned, corporate America knew that it was now boss when it came to accounting. With that, a new era of anything-goes earnings reports – blessed and, in some cases, encouraged by big-name auditors was launched. The licentious behavior that followed quickly became an air pump for the Great Bubble."

"The Great Bubble"

"I know that valuations that don't make sense will come to bad ends. I'm not saying that all of the Internet, or Nasdaq valuations are crazy. But there are a lot that are crazy. Very crazy."

"I don't care if 10,000 people at a cocktail party are making money with Internet stocks. I can't value them."

"It's amazing what you'll see on the markets. We've seen companies valued at tens of billions of dollars that are worth nothing."

"Very few of these companies will be big winners in the long run. It's the nature of capitalism not to get a lot of winners. You get a few."

"We readily acknowledge that there has been a huge
amount of true value created in the past decade by new
or young businesses, and that there is much more to
come. But value is destroyed, not created, by any
business that loses money over its lifetime, no matter
how high its interim valuation may get. What actually
occurs in these cases is wealth transfer, often on a
massive scale. By shamelessly merchandising birdless
bushes, promoters have in recent years moved billions
of dollars from the pockets of the public to their own
purses (and to those of their friends and associates). The
fact is that a bubble market has allowed the creation of
bubble companies, entities designed more with an eye
to making money off investors rather than for them. Too
often, an IPO, not profits, was the primary goal of a
company's promoters. At bottom, the 'business model'
for these companies has been the old-fashioned chain
letter, for which many fee-hungry investment bankers
acted as eager postmen. But a pin lies in wait for every
bubble. And when the two eventually meet, a new wave
of investors learns some very old lessons: First, many
in Wall Street – a community in which quality
control is not prized – will sell investors anything they
will buy. Second, speculation is most dangerous when it
looks easiest."

"Speculation – in which the focus is not on what an asset will produce but rather on what the next fellow will pay for it – is neither illegal, immoral nor un-American. But it is not a game in which Charlie and I wish to play. We bring nothing to the party, so why should we expect to take anything home? The line separating investment and speculation, which is never bright and clear, becomes blurred still further when most market participants have recently enjoyed triumphs. Nothing sedates rationality like large doses of effortless money. After a heady experience of that kind, normally sensible people drift into behavior akin to that of Cinderella at the ball. They know that overstaying the festivities – that is, continuing to speculate in companies that have gigantic valuations relative to the cash they are likely to generate in the future – will eventually bring on pumpkins and mice. But they nevertheless hate to miss a single minute of what is one helluva party. Therefore, the giddy participants all plan to leave just seconds before midnight. There's a problem, though: They are dancing in a room in which the clocks have no hands."

"Far more irrational still were the huge valuations that market participants were then putting on businesses almost certain to end up being of modest or no value. Yet investors, mesmerized by soaring stock prices and ignoring all else, piled into these enterprises. It was as if some virus, racing wildly among investment professionals as well as amateurs, induced hallucinations in which the values of stocks in certain sectors became decoupled from the values of the businesses that underlay them."

"What was at work, also, of course, was market psychology. Once a bull market gets under way, and once you reach the point where everybody has made money no matter what system he or she followed, a crowd is attracted into the game that is responding not to interest rates and profits but simply to the fact that it seems a mistake to be out of stocks. In effect, these people superimpose an I-can't-miss-the-party factor on top of the fundamental factors that drive the market. Like Pavlov's dog, these 'investors' learn that when the bell rings – in this case, the one that opens the New York Stock Exchange at 9:30 a.m. – they get fed. Through this daily reinforcement, they become convinced that there is a God and that he wants them to get rich."

"It's just astounding to me how willing people are in a bull market to toss money around. They think it's easy."

"Certainly, the more people who have never experienced declining prices and who have terrific expectations about great rates of return, if they get disappointed all at once, then I guess it'll be like fire in a crowded theater."

"There's a lot of action and people are day trading and that sort of thing. And, the one piece of advice I'd give is don't do it on borrowed money."

"Because things don't go up forever and a lot of the valuations strike me as extreme and if you own 'em on borrowed money and they go down one day, you know, you don't get to play out your hand."

"It was a mass hallucination, by far the biggest in my lifetime."

"The basic problem was that expectations were too high, and people thought you could make a lot of money without knowing anything, but just basically riding along on hot items."

"We had one of the great bubbles of all time. And people get very happy when they're in bubbles. And it's very tempting, when your neighbor, who you're sure has an IQ 30 points below yours, is making a lot of money to say why can't I make money, too? And it looks so easy, you know, when it's happening. But I've used the analogy that it's like Cinderella at the ball, and you know, you think you're going to leave before midnight, and then you look around and the clock has no hands, and all of a sudden, it turns to pumpkins and mice."

"People behave in extreme ways in markets and over time that's very good for people who keep their heads."

"If I were a business-school professor, as a final exam, I'd give the class an Internet company and ask them how much it's worth. Anyone who answered, I'd flunk."

"What happened is over the last 15 years, stocks have gone up terrifically, in fact, since 1982. There have been two very important drivers of that. One is interest rates have generally gone down and return on equity and businesses have gone up. Those are very good reasons for stocks to go up. After a while, the very act of stocks going up starts drawing in other people who get excited about the fact that their neighbor made a lot of money or maybe they made a little money in the past years and the action of the market itself captures the attention of more and more of the participants as opposed to the businesses themselves. And that's when you get into the dangerous periods."

"I look for businesses in which I think I can predict what they're going to look like in ten or 15 or 20 years. That means businesses that will look more or less as they do today, except that they'll be larger and doing more business internationally. So I focus on an absence of change. When I look at the Internet, for example, I try and figure out how an industry or a company can be hurt or changed by it, and then I avoid it. That doesn't mean I don't think there's a lot of money to be made from that change, I just don't think I'm the one to make a lot of money out of it. Take Wrigley's chewing gum. I don't think the Internet is going to change how people are going to chew gum."

"The best thing is to learn from other guys' mistakes. Patton used to say, 'It's an honor to die for your country; make sure the other guy gets the honor.' There are a lot of mistakes that I've repeated. The biggest one, the biggest category over time, is being reluctant to pay up a little for a business that I knew was really outstanding. The cost of that I think is in the billions, and I'll probably keep making that mistake. The mistakes are made when there are businesses you can understand and that are attractive and you don't do something about them. I don't worry at all about the mistakes that come about like when I met Bill Gates and didn't buy Microsoft or something like that. Most of our mistakes have been mistakes of omission rather than commission."

"The tour we've taken through the last century proves that market irrationality of an extreme kind periodically erupts – and compellingly suggests that investors wanting to do well had better learn how to deal with the next outbreak."

"Despite three years of falling prices, which have significantly improved the attractiveness of common stocks, we still find very few that even mildly interest us. That dismal fact is testimony to the insanity of valuations reached during The Great Bubble. Unfortunately, the hangover may prove to be proportional to the binge. The aversion to equities that Charlie and I exhibit today is far from congenital. We love owning common stocks – if they can be purchased at attractive prices. In my 61 years of investing, 50 or so years have offered that kind of opportunity. There will be years like that again. Unless, however, we see a very high probability of at least 10% pre-tax returns (which translate to 6 1/2-7% after corporate tax), we will sit on the sidelines. With short-term money returning less than 1% after-tax, sitting out is no fun. But occasionally successful investing requires inactivity."

1999

"The numbers on the facing page show just how poor our 1999 record was. We had the worst absolute performance of my tenure and, compared to the S&P, the worst relative performance as well. Relative results are what concern us: Over time, bad relative numbers will produce unsatisfactory absolute results. Even Inspector Clouseau could find last year's guilty party: your Chairman. My performance reminds me of the quarterback whose report card showed four Fs and a D but who nonetheless had an understanding coach. 'Son', he drawled, 'I think you're spending too much time on that one subject.' My 'one subject' is capital allocation, and my grade for 1999 most assuredly is a D. What most hurt us during the year was the inferior performance of Berkshire's equity portfolio – and responsibility for that portfolio, leaving aside the small piece of it run by Lou Simpson of GEICO, is entirely mine. Several of our largest investees badly lagged the market in 1999 because they've had disappointing operating results. We still like these businesses and are content to have major investments in them. But their stumbles damaged our performance last year, and it's no sure thing that they will quickly regain their stride."

"The fallout from our weak results in 1999 was a more-than-commensurate drop in our stock price. In 1998, to go back a bit, the stock outperformed the business. Last year the business did much better than the stock, a divergence that has continued to the date of this letter. Over time, of course, the performance of the stock must roughly match the performance of the business."

"Right now, the prices of the fine businesses we already own are just not that attractive. In other words, we feel much better about the businesses than their stocks. That's why we haven't added to our present holdings. Nevertheless, we haven't yet scaled back our portfolio in a major way: If the choice is between a questionable business at a comfortable price or a comfortable business at a questionable price, we prefer the latter. What really gets our attention, however, is a comfortable business at a comfortable price."

"First, many managers and owners foresaw near-term slowdowns in their businesses – and, in fact, we purchased several companies whose earnings will almost certainly decline this year from peaks they reached in 1999 or 2000. The declines make no difference to us, given that we expect all of our businesses to now and then have ups and downs (Only in the sales presentations of investment banks do earnings move forever upward.) We don't care about the bumps; what matters are the overall results. But the decisions of other people are sometimes affected by the near-term outlook, which can both spur sellers and temper the enthusiasm of purchasers who might otherwise compete with us."

"We made few portfolio changes in 1999. As I mentioned earlier, several of the companies in which we have large investments had disappointing business results last year. Nevertheless, we believe these companies have important competitive advantages that will endure over time. This attribute, which makes for good long-term investment results, is one Charlie and I occasionally believe we can identify. More often, however, we can't – not at least with a high degree of conviction. This explains, by the way, why we don't own stocks of tech companies, even though we share the general view that our society will be transformed by their products and services. Our problem – which we can't solve by studying up – is that we have no insights into which participants in the tech field possess a truly durable competitive advantage. Our lack of tech insights, we should add, does not distress us. After all, there are a great many business areas in which Charlie and I have no special capital-allocation expertise. For instance, we bring nothing to the table when it comes to evaluating patents, manufacturing processes or geological prospects. So we simply don't get into judgments in those fields. If we have a strength, it is recognizing when we are operating well within our circle of competence and when we are approaching the perimeter. Predicting the long-term economics of companies that operate in fast-changing industries is simply far beyond our perimeter. If others claim predictive skill in those industries – and seem to have their claims validated by the behavior of the stock market – we neither envy nor emulate them. Instead, we just stick with what we understand. If we stray, we will have done so inadvertently, not because we got restless and substituted hope for rationality. Fortunately, it's almost certain there will be opportunities from time to time for Berkshire to do well within the circle we've staked out."

Low Tech

"But I will tell you now that we have embraced the 21st century by entering such cutting-edge industries as brick, carpet, insulation and paint. Try to control your excitement."

"But you're right about the low tech. I only buy things I can understand and that really limits things. So, you know, I go into bricks and insulation and all those things that cause you fellows to yawn and go to sleep."

"I haven't got anything against it [hi-tech], it's an important field with a lot of growth possibilities. I just don't know who's going to make money. I do know who's going to make money selling bricks in Texas or candy in California. Incidentally, I know many people in the technology business, and they don't know who's going to be making money 10 years from now either."

"How do you beat Bobby Fischer? You play him at any game but chess. I try to stay in games where I have an edge, and I never will in technology investing."

"I may only understand 10 percent of the businesses in the United States, but as long as I know what 10 percent they are, I'm OK. I try to avoid decisions that put me outside that core area of competence."

"I can understand why somebody buys a Coca-Cola or buys a Gillette razor, and I'm not sure what they're going to click onto on the Internet three years from now."

"By definition, a great company is one that's going to remain great for 30 years. If it's only going to be great for three years, then it ain't a great company."

"A business that must deal with fast-moving technology is not going to lend itself to reliable evaluations of its long-term economics. Did we foresee thirty years ago what would transpire in the television-manufacturing or computer industries? Of course not (Nor did most of the investors and corporate managers who enthusiastically entered those industries). Why, then, should Charlie and I now think we can predict the future of other rapidly-evolving businesses? We'll stick instead with the easy cases. Why search for a needle buried in a haystack when one is sitting in plain sight?"

"I do admire the management of Intel and Microsoft, but I don't have a fix on where they will be in 10 years. I think it is harder to get a fix on those kinds of businesses. I don't know how to value them. And if I started playing around without knowing how to value a company, I might as well buy lottery tickets."

"What I didn't understand was who had permanent competitive advantage, very long-term competitive advantage. I know who has competitive advantage in chewing gum. It's Wrigley's. I know who has competitive advantage in candy in California. It's our brand, See's. I mean, those are the easy things to figure. And you would bet your life on the fact that Gillette would dominate the razor and blade business 10 years from now or that Coke would dominate world-wide the soft drink business. I don't think you'd bet your life on who would dominate some particular aspect of software."

"If you take me out to Silicon Valley, I don't have any interest in doing anything. I could spend a year studying a company, and I wouldn't do a thing out there because I wouldn't understand it. But I understand the Nebraska Furniture Mart."

"I like playing big and fast when I'm comfortable, if I'm not, you won't get me to budge."

"If a business is complex or subject to constant change, we're not smart enough to predict future cash flows."

"It was a business that I could understand. Now, there's all kinds of businesses I can't understand and I try not to buy into those because, why should I expect to make money on something I can't understand? So I'm not in any high tech businesses, for example. But I understand, an ultimate hamburger, a peanut buster or a deli bar and I can handle that. And I like the people that run it. I like the economics of the business. It's a good business. You've got thousands of people that are paying you a royalty for your name of Dairy Queen and the business grows a little every year. It generates cash. The cash gets sent to Omaha and then we go out and buy other businesses with that."

"I've always known reasonably well what I don't know. And there have been all kinds of things I haven't participated in, whether it was semiconductors 20 years ago or whatever it may be. I don't envy other people because they're making money in some manner that I don't understand. If people are speculating in cocoa beans, making a lot of money, it doesn't bother me. And just because I think I know something about a few stocks, doesn't mean I think I know something about all stocks because I don't. So if there are 3000 stocks on the New York Stock Exchange, all I have to do is understand a few of them well. And if I don't understand something, it just doesn't make any difference to me. And so it wasn't that I made a conscious decision to stay away from this or that, it's just I stay away from things I don't think that I understand."

"It's no sin to miss a great opportunity outside one's area of competence."

"I will not abandon an approach whose logic I understand although I find it difficult to apply, even though it may mean forgoing large and apparently easy profits to embrace an approach which I don't fully understand, have not practiced successfully and which could lead to substantial permanent loss of capital."

Derivatives & Other Vehicles

"Charlie and I are of one mind in how we feel about derivatives and the trading activities that go with them: We view them as time bombs, both for the parties that deal in them and the economic system."

"There's no place with as much potential for phony numbers as derivatives."

"In recent years, some huge-scale frauds and near-frauds have been facilitated by derivatives trades. In the energy and electric utility sectors, for example, companies used derivatives and trading activities to report great 'earnings' – until the roof fell in when they actually tried to convert the derivatives-related receivables on their balance sheets into cash. 'Mark-to-market' then turned out to be truly 'mark-to-myth.' I can assure you that the marking errors in the derivatives business have not been symmetrical. Almost invariably, they have favored either the trader who was eyeing a multi-million dollar bonus or the CEO who wanted to report impressive 'earnings' (or both). The bonuses were paid and the CEO profited from his options. Only much later did shareholders learn that the reported earnings were a sham."

"Many people argue that the derivatives reduce systemic problems, in that participants who can't bear certain risks are able to transfer them to stronger hands. These people believe that derivatives act to stabilize the economy, facilitate trade, and eliminate bumps for individual participants. And, on a micro level, what they say is often true. Indeed, at Berkshire, I sometimes engage in large-scale derivatives transactions in order to facilitate certain investment strategies. Charlie and I believe, however, that the macro picture is dangerous and getting more so."

"The derivatives genie is now well out of the bottle, and these instruments will almost certainly multiply in variety and number until some event makes their toxicity clear. Knowledge of how dangerous they are has already permeated the electricity and gas businesses, in which the eruption of major troubles caused the use of derivatives to diminish dramatically. Elsewhere, however, the derivatives business continues to expand unchecked. Central banks and governments have so far found no effective way to control, or even monitor, the risks posed by these contracts."

"In our view, however, derivatives are financial weapons of mass destruction, carrying dangers that, while now latent, are potentially lethal."

"At best a parasite and at worst a cancer on the stream of useful business activity." (Buffett on Program Trading)

"I personally think, before it's all over, junk bonds will live up to their name."
(Said in 1985)

Brokers & Casino-Like Activities

"Brokers, of course, favor new trading vehicles. Their enthusiasm tends to be in direct proportion to the amount of activity they expect. And the more the activity, the greater the cost to the public and the greater the amount of money that will be left behind them to be spread among the brokerage industry. As each contract dies, the only business involved is that the loser pays the winner. Since the casino (the futures market and its supporting cast of brokers) gets paid a toll each time one of these transactions takes place, you can be sure that it will have a great interest in providing very large numbers of losers and winners. But it must be remembered that for the players it is the most clear sort of a 'negative sum game.' Losses and gains cancel out before expenses; after expenses the net loss is substantial. In fact, unless such losses are quite substantial, the casino will terminate operations since the players' net losses compose the casino's sole source of revenue. This 'negative sum' aspect is in direct contrast to common stock investment generally, which has been a very substantial 'positive sum game' over the years simply because the underlying companies, on balance, have earned substantial sums of money that eventually benefit their owners, the stockholders. In my judgment, a very high percentage - probably at least 95% and more likely much higher - of the activity generated by these contracts will be strictly gambling in nature. You will have people wagering as to the short-term movements of the stock market and able to make fairly large wagers with fairly small sums. They will be encouraged to do so by brokers who will see rapid turnover of customers' capital - the best thing that can happen to a broker in terms of his immediate income. A great deal of money will be left behind by these 95% as the casino takes its bite from each transaction. In the long run, gambling-dominated activities that are identified with traditional capital markets, and that leave a very high percentage of those exposed to the activity burned, are not going to be good for capital markets. Even though people participating in such gambling activity are not investors and what they are buying really are not stocks, they still will feel that they have had a bad experience with the stock market."

"Wall Street, unsatisfied by astronomical volume in garden-variety stocks and bonds, has invented new and enticing products for the casino. First came options. These were followed by futures contracts on real financial instruments, such as Treasury bonds. In turn came futures contracts on nonreal items such as market indices. Finally, in the search for an even more exciting and volatile game, Wall Street created options on future index numbers. Predictably, these options are a great favorite. Turnover in stocks is normally calculated on an annual basis; in some of the new esoteric instruments, turnover ranges from 25 percent to 50 percent daily. Brokers, understandably, love such client hyperactivity: the Street's income depends on how often prescriptions are changed, not upon the efficacy of the medicine. But what's good for the croupier, taking his bite out of each transaction, is poison for the patron. Turning from investor into speculator, he suffers the same kind of negative financial effects that befall the person who is converted from making a once-a year bet on the Kentucky Derby to betting all races, every day."

"History shows brokers to be myopic (witness the late Sixties); they often have been happiest when behavior was at its silliest. And many brokers are far more concerned with how much they gross this month than whether their clients – or, for that matter, the securities industry – prosper in the long run."

"The propensity to gamble is always increased by a large prize vs. a small entry fee, no matter how poor the true odds may be. That's why Las Vegas casinos advertise big jackpots and why state lotteries headline big prizes. In securities, the unintelligent are seduced by the same approach in various ways, including: (a) 'penny stocks,' which are 'manufactured' by promoters precisely because they snare the gullible – creating dreams of enormous payoffs but with an actual group result of disaster, and (b) low margin requirements through which financial experience attributable to a large investment is achieved by committing a relatively small stake."

"We do not need more people gambling in nonessential instruments identified with the stock market in this country, nor brokers who encourage them to do so. What we need are investors and advisers who look at the long-term prospects for an enterprise and act accordingly. We need the intelligent commitment of investment capital, not leveraged market wagers. The propensity to operate in the intelligent, pro-social sector of capital markets is deterred, not enhanced, by an exciting casino operating in somewhat the same arena, utilizing somewhat similar language and serviced by the same work force."

"It has always been a fantasy of mine that a boatload of 25 brokers would be shipwrecked and struggle to an island from which there could be no rescue. Faced with developing an economy that would maximize their consumption and pleasure, would they, I wonder, assign 20 of their number to produce food, clothing, shelter, etc., while setting five to endlessly trading options on the future output of the 20?"

"Full-time professionals in other fields, let's say dentists, bring a lot to the layman, but in aggregate, people get nothing for their money from professional money managers."

"They say in this world you can't get something for nothing, but the truth is that money managers in aggregate have gotten something for nothing. I mean they've gotten a lot for nothing. The corollary is that investors have paid something for nothing. That doesn't mean people are evil or that they are charlatans or anything. It's just the nature – you've got a six or seven trillion dollar equity market, and you have a very significant percentage of it managed by professionals, and they charge you significant fees to invest with them, and they have costs when they change around – they cannot do as well as unmanaged money in aggregate. It's the only field in the world that I can think of where the amateur, as long as he is an amateur, will do better than the professional does for the people whose money he's handling."

"We would be willing to take any money management organization in the world managing $10 billion or more, and in the case of brokerage houses, where their brokers in aggregate are handling $10 billion or more, and we would be willing to bet that their aggregate investment experience over the next five years for the group that they advise will be poorer than that achieved by a no-load, very low cost index fund. We'd put up a lot of money to make that wager with anybody who would care to step forward. Gambling may be illegal but now you can do it legally through something called derivatives."

"At the parent company, I can't recall in 38 years ever paying a dime to a consultant."

"If you and I were trading pieces of our business in this room, we could escape transactional costs because there would be no brokers around to take a bite out of every trade we made. But in the real world investors have a habit of wanting to change chairs, or of at least getting advice as to whether they should, and that costs money - big money. The expenses they bear - I call them frictional costs - are for a wide range of items. There's the market maker's spread, and commissions, and sales loads, and 12b-1 fees, and management fees, and custodial fees, and wrap fees, and even subscriptions to financial publications. And don't brush these expenses off as irrelevancies. If you were evaluating a piece of investment real estate, would you not deduct management costs in figuring your return? Yes, of course – and in exactly the same way, stock market investors who are figuring their returns must face up to the frictional costs they bear. And what do they come to? My estimate is that investors in American stocks pay out well over $100 billion a year – say, $130 billion – to move around on those chairs or to buy advice as to whether they should."

"I think investors should stick to buying ownership of businesses. It's not that you can't come up with a theoretical argument for buying, say, a five year option on Coke instead of buying the stock directly. But I think that's a dangerous path to start down, because it's dynamite to start playing with things that can expire worthless or that can be bought with very low margin as are the OEX options you were talking about. Borrowed money frequently leads to trouble. And it's not necessary. If you have to double your money by the end of the year or be shot, then I'd head to the futures market, because you need to do it. Once people start focusing on short-term price behavior, which is the nature of buying calls, LEAPS, or speculating in index futures, you're very likely to take your eye off the main ball, which is just valuing businesses. I don't recommend it."

The Estate Tax

"We have closer to a true meritocracy than anywhere else around the world. You have mobility so people with talents can be put to the best use. Without the estate tax, you in effect will have an aristocracy of wealth, which means you pass down the ability to command the resources of the nation based on heredity rather than merit."

"If we were competing in the Olympics and everybody else chose their team based on heredity or based on their position of influence with the government, and we chose our team based on a bunch of Olympic trials, I think we'd kill everybody in the Olympics."

"All these people who think that food stamps are debilitating and lead to a cycle of poverty, they're the same ones who go out and want to leave a ton of money to their kids."

"I do not believe in the divine right of the womb. These same people are leaving tons of money to their kids. And when those kids emerge from that womb, instead of a welfare officer, they have a trust fund officer."

"The idea that you get a lifetime supply of food stamps based on coming out of the right womb strikes at my idea of fairness."

"There's no reason why future generations of little Buffetts should command society just because they came from the right womb. Where's the justice in that. [Crowd Applauded] My children are here! Are they applauding too?"

"Frankly, I don't think it's right that the quarterback of the Nebraska football team next year should be the eldest son of the quarterback of the Nebraska football team of 22 years ago. Nor do I think that our Olympic team in 2000 should be chosen from the same family that was on the Olympic team in the various respective sports in 1976. We believe in a meritocracy when it comes to athletics and all sorts of things. Now, why not have a meritocracy in terms of what you go out into the world with in terms of the productive goods? Let the resources flow to those who use them best, and then I believe they should give them back to society when they get through."

"One hundred per cent of my stock will go to my wife, if I die first, but on the death of the last of the two of us – and maybe sooner – it will all go to a foundation. That will be it."

"Neither my estate plan nor that of my wife is designed to preserve the family fortune; instead, both are aimed at preserving the character of Berkshire and returning the fortune to society."

"The perfect inheritance is enough money so that heirs feel like they could do anything, but not so much that they feel that they could do nothing."

Money & Politics

"'Market economics' are emerging in the world of political access and influence. This trend has already pushed up prices. But we are far from market equilibrium. For those whose profits are intertwined with government actions, political influence is still ridiculously underpriced. It won't, however, stay that way. If a market model prevails, political clout will eventually be priced appropriately, which means survival of the fattest will be ensured."

"If we instead continue to permit political influence to be dispensed through a market system, we should expect market results. In the private arena, the market works wonders in producing the goods and services that consumer desire. In the public sector, as well, it will deliver to purchasers what they want."

"I think money leads to bad things in politics, and I think that it's bipartisan, incidentally. I think the Republicans and Democrats are both influenced in an equal way by it."

"Well I think absolutely you'll have a government of the wealthy, by the wealthy, and for the wealthy, I mean, it was if you remember Mark Hanna in 1896 who ran McKinley's campaign. They outspent our local hero here in Nebraska, William Jennings Bryan 10 to 1, and somebody afterwards was talking to him about politics, and he said there's only two important things in politics: the first is money and he said 'I can't remember the second one.' So it's been around a long time."

"What could be more foolish than a governing system that rewards undesirable behavior and severely penalizes exemplary conduct? Yet, as deficit-reduction efforts demonstrate, that is precisely the sort of upside-down incentive system that exists in Congress. In the absence of scandal, every senator and representative understands that the gravest threat to his reelection is any vote he casts to either raise taxes or seriously cut spending. He knows, of course, that voters regularly endorse lower deficits as an abstract goal. But he also knows that the specific actions needed to achieve that goal just as regularly anger and energize camps whose votes may prove decisive in the next election. And legislators are understandably reluctant to trade punishment in November for rewards in the hereafter. With every line in the budget and every paragraph in the tax code crucial to some voting group, it's hardly surprising that annual deficits have been rising in relation to GDP, the output of the nation. Our deficits averaged less than 1 percent of GDP in the 1960s, rose to 2 percent in the 1970s and climbed above 4 percent in the 1980s. In the 1990s they are so far running over 5 percent. Clearly, perverse incentives are producing unhealthy results. The solution is to reverse the risks and rewards for our legislators: Enact a constitutional amendment stipulating that every sitting representative and senator becomes ineligible for reelection if in any year of his term our budget deficit runs over 3 percent of GDP. Were this amendment passed, the interests of the nation and the personal interests of our legislators would instantly merge. I do not suggest this amendment because Armageddon has arrived: Our country does not face bankruptcy, and the current national debt, totaling 70 percent of GDP, is not at a proportion that is inconsistent with a healthy economy. But that proportion, up from 33 percent in 1981, is heading in the wrong direction at a fast pace. And fully as threatening are changing demographics that within a few decades are certain to make today's 'tough' choices seem like child's play. Both of these factors mean congressional incentives must be aligned with sensible fiscal behavior – and soon...Clearly, the honor system has failed:There simply aren't enough saints available to staff a large institution that requires its members to voluntarily act against their own well-being. It's time to quit fighting human instincts and instead link that well-being with the fiscal well-being of the country."

Taxation

"I think that generally speaking, a progressive tax system makes great sense in a prosperous country. I was born wired for capital allocation, and that's great in this economy. Wouldn't be worth anything in Bangladesh, it wouldn't have been worth much 300 years ago in the United States, but in the last 50 years, in a market economy, the talent I had paid off enormously. I think that people who are lucky enough to benefit from this society, and believe me, I benefit plenty from this society, I think they should pay a higher part of the common cost of the society. Goodness knows, the rich do not send, disproportionate numbers of people when we go to Afghanistan or to Iraq. I see nothing wrong with those who have been blessed by this society to give a larger proportion of their income to the society than somebody that's working very, very hard to make ends meet."

"I just don't think it's inappropriate in a country like this to have me taxed at 28% if I sell my Berkshire shares, when someone who's trying to find a cure for cancer is taxed at 39%."

"I do think the people that have those skills and get paid enormously well in the market system should pay a bigger toll to society."

"The idea that it creates all kinds of jobs and everything else, that's what sort of turns me off. That's like a manager saying we're going to grow our earnings 20% a year. They don't have the faintest idea, in my view, of how many jobs this is going to create. How could they? Economics is not that precise."
(Buffet on Proposed 2003 Corporate Dividend Tax Cut)

"Supporters of making dividends tax-free like to paint critics as promoters of class warfare. The fact is, however, that their proposal promotes class welfare. For my class."

"This is not a tough tax system for the rich in this country at all."

"I think the tax law is the way to effect behavior. I mentioned during the interim that we in effect have said to insiders who trade in a six month period that they have to give all the profit to the company under the Securities Exchange Act. And that hasn't raised a lot of money for companies but it has certainly modified behavior. I don't think there's anything more effective that gets through faster to investors and to Wall Street generally than the tax law. It was the first thing I read when I got out of school at Columbia when I was 20 years old. And you've got to make it very tight. Because people are going to try and figure out what you use to convert short term to long term and all of that sort of thing."

"One beneficiary of our increased size has been the U.S. Treasury. The federal income taxes that Berkshire and General Re [A Berkshire subsidiary] have paid, or will soon pay, in respect to 1998 earnings total $2.7 billion. That means we shouldered all of the U.S. Government's expenses for more than a half-day. Follow that thought a little further: If only 625 other U.S. taxpayers had paid the Treasury as much as we and General Re did last year, no one else – neither corporations nor 270 million citizens – would have had to pay federal income taxes or any other kind of federal tax (for example, social security or estate taxes). Our shareholders can truly say that they 'gave at the office.' Writing checks to the IRS that include strings of zeros does not bother Charlie or me. Berkshire as a corporation, and we as individuals, have prospered in America as we would have in no other country. Indeed, if we lived in some other part of the world and completely escaped taxes, I'm sure we would be worse off financially (and in many other ways as well). Overall, we feel extraordinarily lucky to have been dealt a hand in life that enables us to write large checks to the government rather than one requiring the government to regularly write checks to us – say, because we are disabled or unemployed."

Terrorism &
Nuclear Weapons

"Ever since 1945, I have believed that the nuclear genie being out of the bottle was the ultimate problem facing mankind."

"The number one problem of mankind, but I don't know how to attack it with money, I think is the spread of nuclear knowledge. I mean I think that the greatest danger that mankind faces is the fact that more and more people will know how to build weapons of incredible destruction and the knowledge won't go away. I don't know how to attack that problem with money."

"The truth is you can't win the war on terrorism. You can win the battles. The threat will be there forever, but you can reduce it. We have got to move that risk to as close to zero as possible."

"That's what terrorism is – you instill fear and make it so that it doesn't go away."

"You get a large number of people who wish us ill, and they always have. And 2000 years ago, if you wished somebody ill, you picked up a rock and threw it at them, and that was the most damage you could do, and 50 years ago you couldn't do much damage. But the people who wish us ill, very few of them will translate that into any sort of attempt at action. But if you look at the spread of knowledge and the materials to do a lot of damage to someone that you wish ill – so that has increased almost exponentially in the last 20 or 30 years, and that goes to nuclear, chemical and biological."

"The probabilities are increasing, in an irregular and immeasurable manner, as knowledge and materials become available to those who wish us ill. Fear may recede with time, but the danger won't – the war against terrorism can never be won. The best the nation can achieve is a long succession of stalemates. There can be no checkmate against hydra-headed foes."

"I don't know if it will happen in 10 years, 10 minutes or 50 years. We are going to have a nuclear incident. It's going to happen, so we are going to have to prepare ourselves for it."

"We estimate our Sept. 11 loss at Berkshire to have been 'only' about $2.3 billion. That's more, by far, than we've ever lost from a single catastrophe, but the toll could have been far larger. Indeed, had a nuclear device been available to Osama bin Laden, the loss could have bankrupted most of the insurance industry, Berkshire very much included. Given that kind of horrendous, but not impossible, nuclear scenario, insured losses could have been $1 trillion, an amount that exceeds the net worth of all property-casualty insurers, worldwide."

"The terrorism risk per dollar of insured value may be 10 or more times for iconic or critical properties in New York City what it is for properties in less-populated areas. But great cities are central to our society. We don't want them to wither under the burden of hugely disadvantageous insurance costs. Indeed, it's in America's interest for them to thrive. Citizens of our leading cities almost certainly bear above-normal physical risks in the war being waged upon us by terrorists. We should not impose crippling economic costs on them as well. In my opinion, we would arrive at a solution for this societal problem if we were to adopt the Federal Deposit Insurance Corp. as a model for where we want to head in the insurance industry."

"Some people will argue that an FDIC model for insurance would be a socialistic intrusion into the private sector. Most surely would have argued the same about the FDIC itself – and yet that institution is today generally regarded as having been enormously beneficial. The problem was once bank runs and economic panics, and we found an innovative solution. Today, the problem is terrorism and its capricious effects on insurance costs, and we need a solution of comparable efficacy."

Public Education

"If you think the cost of a good education system is high, I just invite you to look at the cost of a bad one."

"Public schools are so important to having a society where everyone has half a chance to start at the same starting line. The public school system is a real asset, and I don't think you can get it back if you lose it. You can preserve it. You can't restore it."

"An outstanding public system means that the choice of an alternative education is just that – a choice and not a necessity as it has become in many metropolitan areas. Once a gap develops in the quality of public vs. private schools, it can only widen. The well-to-do will increasingly opt out of an inferior public system, unwilling to sacrifice their own children's education for some abstract ideal. Once that process starts, a vicious spiral begins, with public schools eventually becoming home only to the poor and disadvantaged. When that happens, the well-to-do lose interest in change. The poor lack the power to effect it. Consequently, gross inequities in educational opportunity between these groups become the norm. In short, a first class public school system is like virginity – it can be preserved but not restored. Maybe, some day Americans will learn how to resurrect systems that have disintegrated, but to date it has been impossible."

"If you start one person on the 50-yard line and another person 50 yards back, it's an insult to democracy."

"The public school teacher is probably the most under-compensated and under-appreciated person in the public arena."

"I love anything connected to the public schools. They did wonders for me."

"Next to my parents and wife, the teachers at Rosehill Elementary School had as much to do with my success as anybody."

"I think my seven years at Rosehill were more important than my university years. I could name every teacher I had at Rosehill."

"The smarter the journalists are, the better off society is. To a degree, people read the press to inform themselves – and the better the teacher, the better the student body."

Nebraska

"Talking about Nebraska either as a place to live or a place to work is a no-brainer. Obviously, for the last many decades I could have lived any place in the country that I'd wanted to and conducted business from there – and I've never given a thought to being anyplace but in Nebraska."

"As I go around the country, every time I go someplace, somebody will say, 'Well, do you know so and so? I hear he's from Nebraska.' And I always caution them. I say, you have to be a little careful, because a lot of people claim to be from Nebraska that aren't – It's a status symbol, and so I demand credentials."

"But I'll tell you I never thought for a moment about being anyplace but Nebraska. You could give me first draft pick of all the cities and states in the country, and this is the place I want to be."

"Omaha is as good a spot as any. Here you can see the forest. In New York, it's hard to see beyond the trees."

"I have had far more than my share of good luck in life. High on the list was to be born and to live in Omaha, a stroke of fortune that has aided me in a variety of ways."

"Berkshire Hathaway will be here for many decades to come. I care enormously about Omaha. Berkshire Hathaway is not going anywhere else."

Potpourri

"I'm a long term bull on America. I always have been and always will be."

"There is nothing dumber than betting against America. It hasn't worked since 1776."

"When I was born, the odds of me being born in this country were one in 50. I won the lottery."

"The big thing you want to do is you want to enjoy every day. So you want to have a job you love and you want to work with people that you like and admire and trust. And if you've got that, you're a long way home. I am getting to do exactly what I love to do every single day."

"I tap dance to work every day. I can hardly wait to get there."

"They say success is getting what you want and happiness is wanting what you get. I don't know which one applies in this case, but I do know I wouldn't be doing anything else. I'd advise you that when you go out to work, work for an organization of people you admire, because it will turn you on. I always worry about people who say, 'I'm going to do this for ten years; I really don't like it very well. And then I'll do this...' That's a little like saving up sex for your old age. Not a very good idea."

"I can tell you one quality to look for in a spouse that will allow all your marriages to last. Low expectations."

"It is crazy to do things for your résumé so by the time you are 100, you have the job of your life."

"I work in a job I love. I urge you to work in jobs you love."

"Success is determined by how you feel about your life 50 years from now."

"I tell college students that when you get to be my age, you will be successful if the people you hope to have love you do love you."

"The thing you do not realize is how important your habits are in determining your behavior."

"How I got here is pretty simple in my case. It's not IQ, I'm sure you'll be glad to hear. The big thing is rationality. I always look at IQ and talent as representing the horse-power of the motor, but that the output – the efficiency with which that motor works – depends on rationality. A lot of people start out with 400-horsepower motors but only get a hundred horsepower of output. It's way better to have a 200-horsepower motor and get it all into output. So why do smart people do things that interfere with getting the output they're entitled to? It gets into the habits and character and temperament, and behaving in a rational manner. Not getting in your own way. As I said, everybody here has the ability absolutely to do anything I do and much beyond. Some of you will, and some of you won't. For the ones who won't, it will be because you get in your own way, not because the world doesn't allow you. So I have one little suggestion for you: Pick out the person you admire the most, and then write down why you admire them. You're not to name yourself in this. And then put down that person that, frankly, you can stand the least, and write down the qualities that turn you off in that person. The qualities of the one you admire are traits that you, with a little practice, can make your own, and that, if practiced, will become habit-forming. The chains of habit are too light to be felt until they are too heavy to be broken. I'm stuck. But you will have the habits 20 years from now that you decide to put into practice today. So I suggest that you look at the behavior that you admire in others and make those your own habits, and look at what you really find reprehensible in others and decide that those are things you are not going to do. If you do that, you'll find that you convert all of your horsepower into output."

"Financial success is not a matter of genius. It is a matter of having the right habits."

"Avoid credit cards. Just forget about them. If you start revolving debt on a credit card, you're going to be paying 18 or 20 percent interest. You're not going to make a lot of progress in your financial life."

"When I talk to students – what I always say is to avoid credit card debt. It makes life uphill."

"Nobody's ever gotten rich in this world getting money for 18% to 20%."

"You have to save. It's the only way you're going to acquire wealth unless you hit in the lottery."

"There's nothing wrong with earning 6 or 7 per cent on your money."

"I spend an inordinate amount of time reading. I probably read at least six hours a day, maybe more. I spend an hour or two on the telephone, and the rest of the time I think. We have no meetings at Berkshire. I hate meetings."

"If I was doing it for the money, I would have quit a long time ago."

"I mean all I'm trying to do is buy a piece of a business at an attractive price and the computer doesn't tell me how to do that."

"I spend more hours a week on the computer than Bill Gates does. Of course that's playing bridge."

"Playing bridge is much more fun than making money. I even wouldn't mind going to jail if I could pick my three cellmates."

"What I do is not as tough as being a top-notch bridge player, but both require the ability to see things as they really are."

"I'm quite fond of 1929, since that's when it all began for me. My dad was a stock salesman at the time, and after the Crash came, in the fall, he was afraid to call anyone – all those people who'd been burned. So he just stayed home in the afternoons. And there wasn't television then. Sooo...I was conceived on or about November 30, 1929 (and born nine months later, on Aug. 30, 1930), and I've forever had a kind of warm feeling about the Crash."

"Microsoft has this policy of trying to make their software as user-friendly as possible, so that almost anyone can handle it. In doing that over the years, they've had this chimpanzee that they tested all their new products on. Last week, the chimp died. Bill [Gates], in a panic, called me and said 'We need you, Warren.'"

"You know how our life span depends on how long our parents live? Well, I watch my mother's exercise and diet very carefully. She has 40,000 miles on her bike."

"Someone once said that Wall Street is a parade of innovators, imitators, and swarming incompetents."

"It is close to impossible for outstanding investment management to come from a group of any size."

"Despite our policy of candor, we will discuss our activities in marketable securities only to the extent legally required. Good investment ideas are rare, valuable and subject to competitive appropriation just as good product or business acquisition ideas are. Therefore we normally will not talk about our investment ideas."

"One of the lessons your management has learned – and, unfortunately, sometimes re-learned – is the importance of being in businesses where tailwinds prevail rather than headwinds."

"The airline business before September 11 was a very, very tough business. And the history of the airline business has been terrible. There have been 110 or 120 airlines go bankrupt in the last 25 years. And there's been practically no money made in the airline industry since the Wright Brothers were down there at Kitty Hawk. In fact, if there had been a capitalist down there at Kitty Hawk, he should have shot down Orville and saved us a lot of money."

"The airline business has been extraordinary. It has eaten up capital over the past century like almost no other business because people seem to keep coming back to it and putting fresh money in. You've got huge fixed costs, you've got strong labor unions and you've got commodity pricing. That is not a great recipe for success. I have an 800 number now that I call if I get the urge to buy an airline stock. I call at two in the morning and say, 'my name is Warren, and I'm an aircoholic' and then they talk me down."

"This country will do better per capita in 10 years, in 20 years, in 30 years because it's an incredible economic machine. It's amazing what this machine has turned out. There's been no decade in which our living conditions haven't improved."

"Accounting numbers, of course, are the language of business and as such are of enormous help to anyone evaluating the worth of a business and tracking its progress. Charlie and I would be lost without these numbers: they invariably are the starting point for us in evaluating our own businesses and those of others. Managers and owners need to remember, however, that accounting is but an aid to business thinking, never a substitute for it."

"We look for businesses with fundamentally good economics. That means shying away from commodity-type businesses and from managers we don't have any confidence in."

"Companies such as Coca-Cola and Gillette might well be labeled 'The Inevitables.' Forecasters may differ a bit in their predictions of exactly how much soft drink or shaving-equipment business these companies will be doing in ten or twenty years. Nor is our talk of inevitability meant to play down the vital work that these companies must continue to carry out, in such areas as manufacturing, distribution, packaging and product innovation. In the end, however, no sensible observer - not even these companies' most vigorous competitors, assuming they are assessing the matter honestly - questions that Coke and Gillette will dominate their fields worldwide for an investment lifetime. Indeed, their dominance will probably strengthen. Both companies have significantly expanded their already huge shares of market during the past ten years, and all signs point to their repeating that performance in the next decade. Obviously many companies in high-tech businesses or embryonic industries will grow much faster in percentage terms than will the Inevitables. But I would rather be certain of a good result than hopeful of a great one."

"Coca-Cola sells 47 percent of all the soft drinks in the world. That's 750 million 8-ounce servings a day. That means if you increase the price of Coke one penny, it would add $2.5 billion to the earnings."

"I knew the game was in the bag when I saw that Pepsi was Washington's official drink."
(commenting on Washington v. Nebraska college football game)

"Coke is probably the best large business in the world."

"When you get into consumer products, you're really interested in thinking about what is in the mind of how many people throughout the world think about a product now, and what is likely to be in their mind 5 or 10 or 20 years from now. Now virtually every person around the globe (maybe 75% of people) have some function in their mind about Coca-Cola. The name Coca-Cola means something to them. You know, RC Cola doesn't mean something to virtually anyone in the world. Well, it does to the guy who owns RC, but everybody has something in their mind about Coca-Cola, and overwhelmingly it's favorable. It's associated with pleasant experiences. Now part of that is that by this time, where you are happy, it is at Disneyworld, it's at ballparks, every place you're likely to have a smile on your face, including the Berkshire Hathaway meeting I might add. And that position in the mind is firmly established, and it's established in close to 200 countries around the world. A year from now, it will be established in more minds and will have a slightly different overall position. In 10 years, the position will change just a little bit more. It's share of mind, not share of market that counts. Disney, same way – Disney means something to billions of people. If you're a parent with a couple of young children, and you've got 50 videos that you can buy, you're not going to sit down and preview an hour and a half of each video before deciding which one to stick in front of your kids. And you've got something in mind about Disney that you don't have about ABC Video Company, or you don't even have about 20th Century, and you don't have about Paramount. That name to billions of people has a meaning, and that meaning is overwhelmingly favorable, reinforced by the other activities of the company. Just think what someone would pay to buy that share of mind. You can't do it. You can't do it by a billion dollar advertising budget, or a 3 billion dollar advertising budget, or by hiring twenty thousand supersalesman. So you've got that. Now the question is what does that stand for 5 or 10 or 20 years from now. You know there'll be more people, you know there'll be more people familiar with Disney, and you know that there will always be parents who are interested in having something for their kids to do and that kids will love the same sort of things. That's what you're trying to think about with a consumer products company."

"Another thing I learned in business school was that it doesn't help to be smarter than even your dumbest competitor. The trick is to have no competitors. That means having a product that truly differentiates itself. Say a customer goes into a drugstore and asks for a Hershey bar. The clerk says, 'We don't have any, but why don't you take this other chocolate bar instead; it's a nickel cheaper.' And the customer says, 'I'll go across the street.' It's when the customer will go across the street that you've got a great business."

"I will keep working until about five years after I die, and I've given the directors an Ouija board so they can keep in touch."

"People are not going to stop drinking Coca-Cola if I die tonight, they're not going to quit shaving tonight, they're not going to eat less See's candy, or fewer Dilly Bars, or anything of the sort. Those companies have terrific products, they've got outstanding managers, and all you'll need at the top of Berkshire is someone who can allocate capital and make sure you have the right managers down below. We've got the people identified to do that, and the board of directors of Berkshire knows who they are."

"There are four potential successors to me within the company, but I'd never discuss their names. The truth is that I've got all my net worth safely in Berkshire and I will never sell a share so there is no one more concerned about what happens after my death than I am. I have got this letter which actually goes out the day after I die. It has already been written. And it says that: 'Yesterday I died.' And then it says: 'That's bad news for me, but it's not bad news for you, the shareholders of Berkshire.' And then I go on and explain what is going to happen. I know that is one time when they will be really interested in hearing from me."

"I love running Berkshire, and if enjoying life promotes longevity, Methuselah's record is in jeopardy."

"The beauty of valuing large companies is that it is cumulative. If you started doing it 40 or so years ago, you've really got a working knowledge of an awful lot of businesses. There aren't that many, to start with. What are there, 75 or so important industries? You get to understand how they all operate, and you don't have to start over again every day, and you don't have to consult a computer or anything like that. So, it has the advantage of the accumulation of useful information over time. Why did we decide to buy Coca-Cola in 1988? Well, it may have been because of a couple of small, incremental bits of information, but that came into a mass that had been accumulated over decades. That's why we like businesses that don't change very much."

"When you find a really good business run by first-class people, chances are a price that looks high isn't high. The combination is rare enough, it's worth a pretty good price."

"If we're right on the business, the stock market will take care of itself."

"Buy things you never want to sell. If we need money for something, we'll trim some holdings. But the thing to do with great businesses is to hold on for dear life."

"I've never had a target price or a target holding period on a stock."

"We don't get paid for activity, just for being right. As to how long we'll wait, we'll wait indefinitely."

"We buy everything, even a stock, with the idea that we will hold it forever."

"We look at pricing instead of timing. We price businesses. If we can't get them at prices that make sense, we don't buy them. If you're right about the business, you're going to make money."

"One question I always ask myself in appraising a business is how I would like, assuming I had ample capital and skilled personnel, to compete with it. I'd rather wrestle grizzlies than compete with Mrs. B [Rose Blumkin] and her progeny."

"Maybe grapes from a little eight-acre vineyard in France are really the best in the whole world, but I have always had a suspicion that about 99% of it is in the telling and about 1% in the drinking."

"I don't believe in investing in gold that's dug up out of the ground in South Africa and put back in the ground at Fort Knox."

"If I was bored stiff in Las Vegas, I wouldn't drop a dollar in a slot machine."

"I didn't convert thought into action. I violated the Noah rule: Predicting rain doesn't count, building arks does."

"With enough inside information and $1 million you can go broke in a year."

"Currently liking neither stocks nor bonds, I find myself the polar opposite of Mae West as she declared, 'I only like two kinds of men – foreign and domestic.'"

"There are all kinds of things I don't know about, but you don't have to swing on everything."

"There's nothing more serious than Nebraska football. We have divorces in Nebraska where the husband tells the wife, 'You keep the kids. I want the tickets.'"

"Pension fund managers continue to make decisions with their eyes firmly fixed in the rear-view mirror."

"While investors and managers must place their feet in the future, their memories and nervous systems often remain plugged into the past."

"I'm afraid of any financial services company with an earning-per-share goal. I can't think of anything more dangerous. It leads to cheating and aggressive accounting."

"It's far better to own a portion of the Hope diamond than 100 percent of a rhinestone."

"The idea of buying dollar bills for 40 cents takes immediately to people or it doesn't at all."

"It's no fun being a horse when the tractor comes along, or the blacksmith when the car comes along."

"Risk comes from not knowing what you're doing."

"We're the Metropolitan Museum of Businesses. We promise we'll take care of the paintings and we'll let the painters keep painting them."

"The original purchase of the Berkshire Hathaway textile mill was a terrible mistake – and mine alone. It was a cigar butt investment – free, with a puff left."

"There are probably at least 25 families here in Omaha that have more than $100 million in Berkshire that probably didn't put more than $50,000 in it tops in the past."

"I worry about the expectations getting too high at Berkshire. There's a danger when people get so enthused."

"Eventually, our economic fate will be determined by the economic fate of the business we own."

"I don't know what the soybean crop will be. If somebody makes a lot of money in soybeans, so what? It's not my game."

"'Forecasts', said Sam Goldwyn, 'are dangerous, particularly those about the future.' (Berkshire shareholders may have reached a similar conclusion after rereading our past annual reports featuring your Chairman's prescient analysis of textile prospects)."

"I'm willing to pay more for a good business and for good management than I would 20 years ago. Ben tended to look at the statistics alone. I've looked more and more at the intangibles."

"You can live a full and rewarding life without ever thinking about Goodwill [the accounting term] and its amortization. But students of investment and management should understand the nuances of the subject. My own thinking has changed drastically from 35 years ago when I was taught to favor tangible assets and to shun businesses whose value depended largely upon economic Goodwill. This bias caused me to make many important business mistakes of omission, although relatively few of commission. Keynes identified my problem: 'The difficulty lies not in the new ideas but in escaping from the old ones.' My escape was long delayed, in part because most of what I had been taught by the same teacher had been (and continues to be) so extraordinarily valuable. Ultimately, business experience, direct and vicarious, produced my strong preference for businesses that possess large amounts of enduring Goodwill and that utilize a minimum of tangible assets."

"About seven years ago Frank Rooney, who runs our shoe operations, mentioned he had purchased a sixteenth of a plane and was very satisfied. I had never heard of NetJets before so I looked into it very quickly. I first bought a quarter of a share – 200 hours – for my wife. She's now up to 300 hours. She flies more than Lindbergh ever did."

"Netjets represents by far the most economical way for a great many companies to utilize business aircraft because they are only paying for what they use. We currently are seeing companies which have quite elaborate flight operations change over to a NetJets arrangement and in the process save themselves millions of dollars. My license plate, my daughter bought it for me, says THRIFTY. So I think my reputation is well earned in that respect."

"It is better to point out your own mistakes than have somebody else do it."

"I want to be able to explain my mistakes. This means I only do things I completely understand."

"I'm very suspect of the person who is very good at one business – it also could be a good athlete or a good entertainer – who starts thinking they should tell the world how to behave on everything. For us to think that just because we made a lot of money, we're going to be better at giving advice on every subject – well, that's just crazy."

"To invest successfully, you need not understand beta, efficient markets, modern portfolio theory, option pricing or emerging markets. You may, in fact, be better off knowing nothing of these."

"There seems to be some perverse human characteristic that likes to make easy things difficult."

"Just as is the case in investing, insurers produce outstanding long-term results primarily by avoiding dumb decisions, rather than by making brilliant ones."

"Investing is laying out money today to receive more money tomorrow."

"Investment must be rational; if you can't understand it, don't do it."

"Rationality is essential when others are making decisions based on short-term greed or fear."

"The key to Graham's approach to investing is not thinking of stocks as stocks or part of the stock market. Stocks are part of a business. People in this room own a piece of a business. If the business does well, they're going to do all right as long as they don't pay way too much to join in that business."

"His three basic ideas: look at stocks as businesses; have a proper attitude toward the market; and operate with a margin of safety – they all come straight from Graham."

"You also have to have the knowledge to enable you to make a very general estimate about the value of the underlying businesses. But you do not cut it close. That is what Ben Graham meant by having a margin of safety. You don't try and buy businesses worth $83 million for $80 million. You leave yourself an enormous margin. When you build a bridge, you insist it can carry 30,000 pounds, but you only drive 10,000 pound trucks across it. And that same principle works in investing."

"In assessing risk, a beta purist will disdain examining what a company produces, what its competitors are doing, or how much borrowed money the business employs. He may even prefer not to know the company's name. What he treasures is the price history of its stock. In contrast, we'll happily forgo knowing the price history and instead will seek whatever information will further our understanding of the company's business. After we buy a stock, consequently, we would not be disturbed if markets closed for a year or two. We don't need a daily quote on our 100% position in See's or H.H. Brown to validate our well-being. Why, then, should we need a quote on our 7% interest in Coke? In our opinion, the real risk that an investor must assess is whether his aggregate after-tax receipts from an investment (including those he receives on sale) will, over his prospective holding period, give him at least as much purchasing power as he had to begin with, plus a modest rate of interest on that initial stake. Though this risk cannot be calculated with engineering precision, it can in some cases be judged with a degree of accuracy that is useful. The primary factors bearing upon this evaluation are: 1) The certainty with which the long-term economic characteristics of the business can be evaluated; 2) The certainty with which management can be evaluated, both as to its ability to realize the full potential of the business and to wisely employ its cash flows; 3) The certainty with which management can be counted on to channel the rewards from the business to the shareholders rather than to itself; 4) The purchase price of the business; 5) The levels of taxation and inflation that will be experienced and that will determine the degree by which an investor's purchasing-power return is reduced from his gross return. These factors will probably strike many analysts as unbearably fuzzy, since they cannot be extracted from a data base of any kind. But the difficulty of precisely quantifying these matters does not negate their importance nor is it insuperable. Just as Justice Stewart found it impossible to formulate a test for obscenity but nevertheless asserted, 'I know it when I see it,' so also can investors - in an inexact but useful way - 'see' the risks inherent in certain investments without reference to complex equations or price histories."

Closing Remarks

"If I were to give credit in terms of how I've done it in investments, my Dad would be number one, and Ben Graham would be number two. Charlie Munger would be number three."

"My dad was the super-hero of all time to me. My dad said anything you do that is legitimate, I'm for it. He didn't say you've got to do what I do or anything of that sort. He might have been more pleased if I'd been a minister or something, but he supported me 100 per cent."

"He taught me to do nothing that could be put on the front page of a newspaper. I have never known a better human being than my Dad."

"You tell me who somebody's heroes are, and I will tell you how they will turn out."

"You people in this room are lucky. You had a 1-in-30 chance of being born in the United States. In 1930, when I was born, I had a 1-in-50 chance of being born in the United States. I had a 50 percent chance of being born male. And I had a 1 percent chance of being born male in the United States."

"Let's say that it was 24 hours before you were born, and a genie appeared and said, 'You look like a winner. I have enormous confidence in you, and what I'm going to do is let you set the rules of the society into which you will be born. You can set the economic rules and the social rules, and whatever rules you set will apply during your lifetime and your children's lifetimes.' And you'll say, 'Well, that's nice, but what's the catch?' And the genie says, 'Here's the catch. You don't know if you're going to be born rich or poor, white or black, male or female, able-bodied or infirm, intelligent or retarded.' So all you know is that you're to get one ball out of a barrel with, say, 5.8 billion balls in it. You're going to participate in what I call the ovarian lottery. It's the most important thing that will happen to you in your life, but you have no control over it. It's going to determine far more than your grades at school or anything else that happens to you. Now, what rules do you want to have? I'm not going to tell you the rules, and nobody will tell you; you have to make them up for yourself. But they will affect how you think about what you do in your will and things of that sort. That's because you're going to want to have a system that turns out more and more goods and services. You've got a great quantity of people out there, and you want them to live pretty well, and you want your kids to live better than you did, and you want your grandchildren to live better than your kids. You're going to want a system that keeps Bill Gates and Andy Grove and Jack Welch working long, long after they don't need to work. You're going to want the most able people working more than 12 hours a day. So you've got to have a system that gives them an incentive to turn out the goods and services. But you're also going to want a system that takes care of the bad balls, the ones that aren't lucky. If you have a system that is turning out enough goods and services, you can take care of them. You don't want people worrying about being sick in their old age, or fearful about going home at night. You want a system where people are free of fear to some extent. So you'll try to design something, assuming you have the goods and services to solve that sort of thing. You'll want equality of opportunity – namely a good public school system – to make you feel that every piece of talent out there will get the same shot at contributing. And your tax system will follow from your reasoning on that. And what you do with the money you make is another thing to think about. As you work through that, everybody comes up with something a little different. I just suggest you play that little game."

A woman once approached Warren Buffett and told him 'My only regret is that my two children are girls, so I couldn't name them Warren.' 'How about a Warranella?', Buffett replied.

"Mr. Buffett, I presume. May I call you Warren? I mean you and me alone together, oh, Warren, Warren, you are my destiny."
(Susan Lucci to Warren Buffett in All My Children Episode)

NOTE

Many of these quotations have been culled from Warren Buffett's Berkshire Hathaway annual reports from 1977 to 2002. All of these reports in their entirety are accessible on the website berkshirehathaway.com. These quotes are just a few nuggets panned from the annual reports and are no substitute for reading the annual reports, which provide a cornucopia of knowledge and information.